A TREASURY OF
CLASSICAL
MYTHOLOGY

A TREASURY OF
CLASSICAL
MYTHOLOGY

A.R. Hope Moncrieff

BARNES
&NOBLE
BOOKS
NEW YORK

ISBN 1-56619-119-X

Printed and bound in Singapore

Apotheosis of Homer (right). A vase
modelled by Flaxman. (Wedgwood
Museum, Staffordshire, England.) The
great epic poet, Homer, lived in
classical Greece around 850 B.C.

Jupiter and Thetis (previous page), by
Jean-Augustè Dominique Ingres. Oil
on canvas, 327 3 260 cm, 1811. (Musée
Granet, Aix-en-Provence, France.)
The Nereid, Thetis, appeals to Jupiter,
father of the gods.

CONTENTS

INTRODUCTION

This volume is an abridged version of A.R. Hope Moncrieff's *Classic Myth and Legend*. As the author states in the original preface, it "deals with the famous legendary fictions of Ancient Greece that have furnished so many themes and allusions to modern authors".

Passed down orally from generation to generation over several thousand years, these ancient stories were eventually committed to written form. They were then taken up by later Greek poets and playwrights, and thus passed down through the centuries to us today.

Hope Moncrieff declares that his task has been "to reproduce the chief features of this mythology, usually after the best-known version, yet sometimes with an eye to the taste of readers who will not so readily stomach the grossness that did not offend ancient hearers. In a certain amount of selection or suppression, one is justified by classic example; but, as far as may be, the attempt is to present the Greek mind as shown in its famous fables, and to make familiar the names and characters so often cited in poetry, oratory and history."

There is no doubt that Greek mythology, with its sweeping cast of gods and semi-gods, heroes and mortals, wood and water nymphs, monsters of land and sea, the heights of Olympus and the depths of Hades, owes much to Greek genius and imagination. The very tradition of such stories, however, reaches back beyond the time of their first telling to a pre-Hellenic past.

The two great epics of Greek mythology are of course those recorded by Homer in his *Iliad*, describing the Trojan war, and in the *Odyssey*, which traces the adventures of Odysseus on his perilous journey home.

Hermes (Mercury), was the youthful messenger of the gods, swift and silver-tongued, deity of travellers and traders, speakers and writers. Attributed to Francesco Righetti, after Giambologna. Bronze, 177 cm high, 1603–1616. (National Gallery of Art, Washington.)

Venus, Cupid and Mars (opposite), by Luca Giordana, 1632–1705. (Museum of Capodimonte, Naples, Italy.) A revealing contrast between Mars (Ares), the fierce and powerful god of war, Venus (Aphrodite), the sweet and beautiful goddess of love, and Cupid (Eros), the charming and mischievous son of Venus.

A Youth on a gravestone stele or tablet. Marble, 109 cm high, *c.* 420 B.C. Found at Salamis, Greece. (National Museum of Athens.)

Frieze detail from the Parthenon, 447–432 B.C. (Acropolis Museum, Athens.) The Parthenon, part of the Athens Acropolis, was erected to Athena, patron goddess of Athens.

Homer wrote down these tales in 8,000 B.C. – four hundred years after the Trojan war took place. From Homer and his near-contemporary Hesiod, these themes, and many other classical myths from unknown sources, were retold in the plays of Aeschylus and Sophocles, in Ovid's *Metamorphoses*, Plutarch's *Parallel Lives*, Pindar's *Odes* and Pausanias's *Descriptions of Greece*, among others.

The result, writes Hope Moncrieff, was that "we may have similar exploits recorded of different personages and varying, often contradictory, versions of what seems the same tale. That, of course, is no new thing in mythology. The classical writers who had to handle this medley of tradition were more or less free to 'edit' it according to their own tastes and prejudices . . . Hercules appears a contemporary of many heroes, some of whom must have been too old or too young to be very serviceable among the Argonaut crew that had him for a shipmate."

Hope Moncrieff's lyrical style in these tales echoes the very lyricism and poetry with which the epic myths were originally told. For all their fantastical nature and the suspension of disbelief that their reading demands, these are stories whose themes still very much apply today – human endeavour, perseverance and the spirit of adventure, love and hatred, bravery and cowardice, jealousy, devotion, temptation, revenge and just deserts.

A complete roll-call of all of the *dramatis personae* of Greek mythology cannot be attempted here. However, the following list gives fourteen of the most prominent characters, with such details as are so well-documented as to be generally accepted as "facts". The parentage, characteristics, triumphs and failures of the most important protagonists are revealed as the individual stories unfold, but first we rejoin Hope Moncrieff's narrative in his description of the Pantheon.

The Pantheon

The poets generally recognise between twelve and sixteen great gods and goddesses, their rule over man and nature interrupted only by their own feuds. (They did, however, occasionally bow to a Fate mistily conceived as lord of all life, human and supernatural.) The following list of these divine personages gives their main title first and the more familiar names of the Latin deity in brackets afterwards.

ZEUS (Jupiter, Jove) was the king of earth and air and overlord of Olympus, yet even he was not wholly free from the power of Fate. He figures as a magnificent form, white-haired and bearded, sometimes crowned with oak leaves, holding in his hands the thunderbolts with which he scourged impiety. An eagle attends him as minister of his will and for page or cup-bearer he has Ganymede, a boy so beautiful that Zeus had him stolen from Mount Ida to make him immortal in heaven.

HERA (Juno), wife of Zeus, was the legitimate queen of Olympus. Through her jealousy she led her husband a troubled life. Her other characteristics were pride and self-satisfaction and always she proved quick to take offence at any slight on the part of gods or men. Her handmaid was Iris, the rainbow, who carried her messages to earth. Her daughter Hebe served with Ganymede as cup-bearer at the celestial table.

APOLLO (with Phoebus prominent among his many aliases) was the most beautiful and the most beloved of the Olympians. Beside his sister Selene, the moon, he figures as Helios, the sun, and was sometimes also known as Hyperion. He was the son of Zeus and Leto (Latona), who was driven to Delos by the jealousy of Hera (Juno). Because of Hera's continuing persecution of his mother, Apollo was reared by Themis, and thrived so well in this setting that at his first taste of nectar and ambrosia he burst his swaddling-clothes and stood forth a fully-grown youth, demanding the lyre and the silver bow with which he is usually represented.

ARTEMIS (Diana), Apollo's twin sister, also had several aliases. One was the renowned Diana of the Ephesians, whose temple ranked among the Seven Wonders; another was the cruel goddess Tauris. The Arcadian Artemis was a goddess of hunting and wildlife. She was chaste to a fault and her fatal jealousy was more easily aroused not by love, but by presumption on the part of mortals.

ATHENE (Minerva) was another virgin goddess. Her chief title, however, shows her affinity with the city that honoured her with the renowned Parthenon. She is held to have sprung fully-grown and armed from the head of her father Zeus. She is often represented in armour and so has passed for the goddess of war; her true spirit, however, was for invention, the arts and crafts and woman's handiwork. The animals sacred to her were the serpent, the cock and the owl.

APHRODITE (Venus), the goddess of love, was a daughter of Zeus according to one story, though an older myth suggests that she sprung from the sea. Her name, "foam-born", bears out such an origin. She was endowed with all the charms of feminine grace and beauty.

CUPID (the Greek Eros, but best known by his Latin name) was the son of Venus. Poets and artists have made much of this wanton imp, naked and winged, his eyes sometimes blindfolded. His torch kindled hearts, and the arrows he shot in careless mischief were sometimes tipped with gold to quicken the heart, and sometimes with lead to palsy the pulse of love.

Apollo of Veio, terracotta, *c.* 500 B.C. (Villa Giuglia, Rome.) Apollo, son of Zeus and Leto, was the god of the sun, of the arts and of healing. He was the most classically Greek of the gods, typifying the ancient ideal of physical and intellectual perfection.

Jupiter and Juno on Mount Ida, by James Barry, 1741–1806. Canvas, 101 × 127 cm. (City Art Galleries, Sheffield, England.) Jupiter and Juno were the Roman counterparts of the Greek gods, Zeus and Hera, father and mother of all the Olympian gods and goddesses.

11

Hephaestus (Vulcan), was the Grecian god of fire and craft. Though lame and awkward, he was a gifted craftsman who fashioned things of wonder in his workshop with the anvil and twenty bellows which worked spontaneously at his bidding.

HEPHAESTUS (Vulcan) was the god of fire, in its industrial applications. This lame and ugly fellow played the low comedian of Olympus – at his hobbling gait the more elegant gods often burst into unextinguishable laughter. Rough and begrimed as he was, there could be no question of his usefulness. For the heroes of myth he fashioned such masterpieces as the shield of Hercules, the armour of Achilles and the sceptre of Agamemnon. His workshops naturally were placed in volcanic islands, where the Cyclops acted as his journeymen.

ARES (Mars), son of Zeus and Hera, was the god of war. In Greek mythology, this blustering athlete cuts no noble figure, showing something of the savage sullenness and stupidity that came naturally to legendary giants. Mars rose to a loftier position at Rome.

HERMES (Mercury) was another son of Zeus. His special function was as messenger and herald of the gods, in which capacity he is represented as a handsome and agile youth, with winged sandals and a broad-brimmed hat, also winged. Hermes came to be looked on as the god of herds, and also of commerce and of theft, a natural enough connection when cattle were the standard of value. He was also the guardian of roads, of clever inventions, of games of chance and a multitude of other apparently unrelated aspects of daily life!

The Wedding of Psyche (left), by Giulio Romano. All the gods and goddesses, even Aphrodite, blessed the happy pair. Fresco, 1528. (Sala di Psiche, Palazzo del Te, Mantua, Italy.)

Athena (below). Stele, *c.* 450 B.C. (Acropolis Museum, Athens.) Athena, the great goddess of wisdom, presided over the whole intellectual and moral side of human life. She was especially the presiding deity of Attica and of Athens which bears her name.

POSEIDON (Neptune), brother of Zeus, was god of the sea, under which he had a marvellous golden palace, its grottos adorned with corals and sea-flowers, and lit with a phosphorescent glow. His sceptre was the trident and he rose forth in a chariot drawn by dolphins, sea-horses or other marine creatures.

PLUTO, lord of the underworld, King of the dead, was the most dreadful of the gods, conceived as a dark-browed form, seated on an ebony throne or driving a chariot drawn by coal-black steeds. He brandished a two-pronged spear and among his possessions was a helmet that had the power to cast a spell of invisibility.

DIONYSUS (Bacchus), a son of Zeus, was ever youthful, handsome and effeminate. Clad in a panther skin, he was crowned with vine leaves and grape bunches and carried a wand wreathed with ivy or vines. He was a god who came to Greece with the culture of the vine, and brought along with him eastern orgies, which also had their religious side.

PLUTUS, the god of wealth, was a different personage from Pluto. The ancients had him blinded by Zeus, and poets and moralists, passing on the story throughout the ages, continued to point out that riches do not always go with merit.

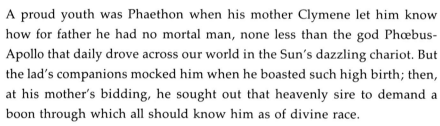

Eos, or Aurora.

Eos (right), the goddess of dawn, was daughter of Hyperion and Theia. At the close of every night, she rose from her sleep, and ascended to heaven to announce the coming of the light. From *Manual of Mythology* by A.S. Murray, 1873, London.

Charioteer, bronze, 180 cm high. Chariot-racing was a popular sport in ancient times. Chariots were also commonly used in battle. From the sanctuary of Apollo at Delphi, *c*. 470 B.C. (Museum of Delphi.)

PHAETHON

A proud youth was Phaethon when his mother Clymene let him know how for father he had no mortal man, none less than the god Phœbus-Apollo that daily drove across our world in the Sun's dazzling chariot. But the lad's companions mocked him when he boasted such high birth; then, at his mother's bidding, he sought out that heavenly sire to demand a boon through which all should know him as of divine race.

Before dawn he came to the golden palace of Phœbus, where the purple-mantled god sat on his ivory throne, amid a rainbow sheen of jewels. Round him stood his ministers and henchmen, the Hours, the Days, the Months, and noblest of all, the Seasons: Spring wreathed with fresh blossoms, naked Summer clothed in leaves and crowned with ears of corn, Autumn stained by the clusters of fruit he held in his sunburnt arms, and shivering Winter with snow-white locks. Phaethon's eyes were dazzled before such magnificence, so that he durst not approach the throne till his all-seeing father called him by name.

"Welcome, my son, to the halls of heaven!" quoth Phœbus, laying aside the crown of sunrays on which mortal sight could not bear to gaze. "But say, what brings thee from earth?"

Thus encouraged, the beardless boy drew near to falter out his request, and soon waxed bolder in the god's smiling face. He made his complaint that men would not believe him Apollo's son, unless his father gave him a pledge of his birth that might be seen by the whole world.

"Before the whole world," cried the god, "will I own thee for my son. Well hast thou done to seek a proof of favour, which thy father grants unheard: so I swear by the Styx, that oath that binds even the gods. Ask, then, and have!"

"Father," exclaimed Phaethon eagerly, "grant me my dearest wish, for one day to be trusted to drive the chariot of the Sun!"

A shade fell on the radiant face of Phœbus, and once and again he shook his glowing head before he answered.

"Rash boy, that knows not what he would dare! That charge is too great for heedless youth, nay, for any mortal, since not even to the gods may it be safely committed. Jupiter himself takes not in hand the reins of the Sun's coursers. Among all the sons of Olympus, I alone can stand firm in the burning car and rule aright its fiery steeds on their steep and toilsome path. Renounce, I beseech thee, such a perilous boon. Ask anything else in heaven or earth, and again I swear by Styx it is thine."

But the forward youth, with pouts and entreaties, held fast to his audacious wish, and would not let himself be moved by fatherly counsels. So at last, the lord of the Sun, bound by his oath, was fain to consent, though sorely fearing what would come of trusting such strong steeds to so weak a hand.

It was time to be off on that daily journey, for already Aurora began to draw back the rosy curtains of the East, as Phœbus led his son to Vulcan's masterpiece, the golden chariot studded with sparkling gems, all so rich and beautiful that Phaethon's head was turned by his good fortune to be its master for one day. The vanishing of the stars and the fading of the moon's horns were signal to lead out the four coursers of the Sun, pawing and neighing to show how, full fed with ambrosia, and refreshed by the night's rest, they came eager for their accustomed task. While the swift-fingered Hours fitted on their clanking bits, and harnessed them to the chariot-pole, fond Phœbus anointed the youth with a sacred balm that would enable him better to bear the heat of his glowing course. Meanwhile shining Apollo plied Phaeton with warnings, to which his impatient son hardly gave ear.

"Keep heedfully the straight path marked by fearsome signs of beasts. Beware in going by the horns of the Bull and the mouth of the roaring Lion, and the far-stretched claws of the Scorpion or the Crab. Shun the South Pole and the North Pole; hold the upper arch of the sky from east to west; safest ever is the middle way. Sink not too far down, lest the earth catch fire; rise not too high to scorch the face of heaven. Spare the goad, and draw tight the reins, for my horses fly of themselves, and all the labour is to hold them in. Now mount the car—or no, dear son, bethink thee in time! It is not honour thou shalt win, but punishment and destruction. Leave the chariot to me, and be content to watch its course like thy fellow men!" Apollo beseeched his son.

But already the presumptuous stripling had sprung up to grasp the reins; and when Thetis drew the bar of heaven, he let the chafing horses bound forth, throwing back a hasty word of thanks and farewell to his anxious father.

Boldly Phaethon urged that mettlesome team through the morning mists, with the east wind following to sweep him on his proud career. But soon the swiftness took away his breath, while under his light weight the car shook and swayed like a keel without ballast, till his head began to turn. And too soon the fiery coursers felt how their reins were in an unpractised hand. Rearing and starting aside, they left their wonted way; then all the earth was amazed to see the glorious chariot of the Sun

Statue and Temple of Apollo, Pompeii. Photographed by Edwin Smith, *c.* 1960. Overwhelmed by volcanic larva in A.D. 79, a great part of the ancient city was well preserved. Much has now been excavated, yielding valuable archaeological information, and throwing light on the private life of the ancients.

The Three Horae (above), the blooming daughters of Zeus and Themis, and goddesses of the seasons. From *Manual of Mythology* by A.S. Murray, 1873, London.

The Fall of Phaeton (right) by Michelangelo, black chalk, 41 × 23 cm, 1533. (Royal Library of Windsor Castle, © Her Majesty the Queen, 1992.) "Down the youth dashed with blazing locks, swift as a falling star."

speeding crookedly overhead as a flash of lightning. Before he had gone far, the rash charioteer sorely repented his ambition, and would have asked no greater boon than to be saved from that perilous honour. Too late he saw how wisely his father had warned him. His head whirled, his face grew white, and his knees shook as he looked to earth and sea spread out beneath, and to the boundless sky above. In vain he tugged at the tangled

bridles; in vain he cried to the horses which he could not call by name. Heated by the wild course, they no longer minded his unmasterful hand, but took their own way through the air, prancing hither and thither at will. Now they soared up towards the sky, so that the clouds began to smoke, and the Moon looked out with dismay to see her brother's car so strangely guided. Then turning downwards, as if to cool themselves in the ocean, they passed close over a high mountain, that in a moment burst into flames.

Thus fearsome disaster fell upon the earth. The Sun, instead of holding his stately beneficent course across the sky, seemed to rush down in wrath like a meteor, blasting the fair face of nature and the works of man. The grass withered; the crops were scorched away; the woods went up in fire and smoke; then beneath them the bare earth cracked and crumbled, and the blackened rocks burst asunder under the heat. The rivers dried up or fled back to their hidden fountains; the lakes began to boil; the very sea sank in its bed, and the fishes lay gasping on the shore, unless they could gain the depths whence Poseidon thrice raised his head and thrice plunged back into his shrinking waves, unable to bear the deadly glow. Scythia was not shielded by its frosts, nor Caucasus by its snows, licked up beneath the passage of that scorching whirlwind. Mighty Atlas, they say, had all but let the red-hot world fall from his writhing shoulders. On that day the negroes were burned black, and, ever since, one stretch of our earth has lain a sandy desert, where neither man nor beast can thrive. But all over the habitable world the Sun's charioteer spread woe and ruin, as its cities were consumed one by one, and the people in their torment swarmed here and there, like ants, among the ashes of their homes. Never had such a calamity fallen on man since Zeus and Poseidon drowned man's impiety under the flood in which only Deucalion and Pyrrha found dry land!

By now the wretched Phaethon had given up hope to check or guide his baleful course. Blinded by terror and by the glare spreading beneath him wherever he sped, seared by the heat till he could not stand on the glowing car, he threw down the useless reins, to fall on his knees with a pitiful prayer for his father's help. But his prayer was lost in the cry that went up from the whole earth, calling upon the lord of heaven to save mankind from destruction.

Not unheard rose that cry. All-powerful Zeus was sleeping away the noonday hour; but quickly he awoke and raised his head and saw what had befallen. Snatching a thunderbolt that lay ready to his hand, he hurled it through the smoky air, and struck senseless Phaethon from this chariot he could not control. Down the youth dashed with blazing locks, swift as a falling star, to be quenched like a firebrand in the river Eridanus. Then the horses of the Sun shook off their yokes, breaking loose to seek their stalls in the sky; and for once at noon night fell upon the earth, lit only by the flickering fires kindled through Phaethon's folly.

So, on that woeful day, ended the vainglorious son born to Phœbus-

Phaeton and Apollo, by Giovanni Battista Tiepolo, 1696–1770. Oil on canvas. (Akademie der Bildenen Kunste, Vienna.) Phaeton, Apollo's son, was dashed to the earth after his hapless and reckless ride in his father's sun-chariot.

Apollo, who was fain to hide his countenance for shame of his fatherly fondness. But some there were who mourned the rash youth's end. When the nymphs of the Eridanus had buried him on its banks, his mother, frantic with grief, came thither to pour out her heart's blood in sorrow. His three sisters, too, wept so bitterly that the pitying gods changed them into poplar trees dropping tears of amber upon the water. And his friend Cygnus dived so often into the river to gather up Phaethon's charred members that, when he pined away for grief, it was granted him still to haunt the stream in the shape of a swan.

PERSEUS
The Gorgon

Acrisius, king of Argos, was sore troubled through an oracle declaring that by the hand of a grandson he should die; then, having but one child, his fair daughter Danaë, he thought to cheat that doom by keeping her unwedded. To make sure, he shut her up in close prison, a cave underground, or, as some say, a brazen tower, never to see the face of man while she lived. But Danaë was visited by Zeus in the form of a shower of gold, and here she bore a son, who was to be the famous hero Perseus.

When the infant's crying came to the ears of the king, and he learned how a grandson had been born to him for all his watchfulness, his cowardly soul was filled with dismay. Not daring to kill the boy, nor yet to let him live, he had mother and child put together in a chest and sent drifting out to drown or starve upon the stormy sea. But Zeus watched over them; and at his bidding Poseidon stilled the winds and waves that gently bore their frail ark eastward, till it came washed ashore on the island of Seriphos in the Ægean archipelago.

Here Danaë and her babe were found by a fisherman named Dictys, who treated them kindly, and took them to his house to bring up Perseus as his own child. And so well throve this young stranger that the men of Seriphos could guess him to be of royal birth, nay, son of a god. In sports and combats he soon vanquished all his playfellows, and grew up to full strength and stature, his mind set on brave deeds by which he might prove himself a hero among men. In dreams he was inspired by Athene, who strung his heart to choose the deadliest perils in the flower of youth, rather than inglorious ease and safety.

Soon he was to have his desire. His foster-father Dictys had a brother, Polydectes, the chief of the island, but of less noble nature. He, at first friendly to the strangers cast on his shore, came to love Danaë, and would have forced her to be his wife. But all her heart was given to her son, and such a wooer seemed unworthy of one who had been loved by a god. The cunning Polydectes bethought him how to get rid of this manly youth who stood as a guard to his mother's honour. To have Danaë in his power he

Danae and the Baby Perseus Adrift at Sea. Zeus watched over them and stilled the winds and waves. From *The Heroes* by Charles Kingsley, 1868, London.

The Call of Perseus to Slay Medusa, by E. Burne-Jones. Body colour and mixed media, 150 × 126 cm, 1876–1885. (Southampton City Art Gallery, England.)

set Perseus upon a fearful adventure, from which the bravest man was little likely to come back alive.

Danae and the Golden Rain, by Titian, oil on canvas, 135 × 152 cm, 1554. (Kunsthistorisches, Vienna.) Imprisoned by her father, Danae was visited by Zeus in the form of a golden shower.

The task given him was to slay the monster Medusa, one of the three Gorgon sisters, she alone of them mortal, but her very looks deadly to the best-armed foe. For, to punish an impious outrage on Athene, her hair had been turned into vipers writhing about a face so horrible that whoever set eyes upon it was stiffened to stone before he could strike a blow. Yet Perseus did not fear to face the Gorgon, when his patron Athene gave him wise counsels how he should accomplish that perilous quest.

"Not without help of the gods can the bravest man assail such a foe," she bid him know, when the bold youth would have made light of all he must dare. For now the goddess appeared to him in radiant majesty, accompanied by her brother Hermes, and they lent him certain powerful talismans in proof of their favour. Hermes girded on to him his own crooked sword that could cut through the stoutest armour, and fitted the youth's feet with his winged sandals to bear him swiftly over land and sea. Moreover, from the realm of Pluto he brought him a wonderful helmet that made the wearer of it invisible. Athene gave him her polished shield, which he must use like a mirror so as to strike Medusa without looking straight in her horrific face. Also she provided him with a goatskin bag to hide the Gorgon's head, that even in death would freeze the blood of all who beheld it.

Perseus and the Graiae, by E. Burne-Jones. Body colour and mixed media, 152 × 170.5 cm, 1876–1885. (Southampton City Art Gallery, England.) "Dim, shapeless, with one tooth and one eye between them . . ."

The Lion Gate at Mycenae, c. 1250 B.C. An ancient town in Argolis, Mycenae was probably built in very early times as a military outpost. Legend has it that it was founded by Perseus, and was the city of Agamemnon, "abounding in gold".

Thus equipped, he was bidden first to seek out, in their icy home of the north, the frostbound Graiæ, half-sisters of the Gorgons, who alone could tell him the way to the far-off isle where Medusa had her lair. Not an hour did he lose in setting forth, only begging of Athene to watch over his mother till he brought back Medusa's head. With such heavenly aid, he could make no doubt of victory.

Springing into the air from the cliffs of Seriphos, lightly he flew to the north, till he came among snows and mists and mountains of ice where no mortal man can dwell. There, on the edge of the Hyperborean sea, he found the Grey Sisters huddled up together, dim and shapeless forms, of which his eyes could hardly tell whether they were two or three. Clothed only in their long hair, white and bristling with ice, so old were they and so doting that they had but one eye and one tooth left between them, which their fumbling hands passed from each to other with groans and murmurs, as in turn they needed to munch the snowflakes or to peer through the blinding mists. This Perseus know from Athene; and as she had bidden him, he stole up to the old hags, invisible in his helm of darkness, then suddenly snatched away their eye, as they wrangled which should have it to see whose steps came clanging on the frosty shore.

"Tell me the way to the Gorgons," demanded he, "or I take your tooth also, and leave you to starve in this wilderness."

A miserable outcry those Grey Sisters made, when they found themselves thus robbed by an unseen hand. With threats and curses they bid him give up their eye; but he held it firm, till, since so it must be, they mumbled out directions by which he might find the Gorgons' Isle. For thanks he gave them back their eye, but they saw him not, for he was gone before they could nod their feeble heads, falling asleep like blocks of ice.

Now he must fly far to the south, where the mists and snows soon melted away, and the earth lay green with fields and forests, and the blue sea shone and sparkled under a glowing sky. Hot and hotter grew the air as he flew over land and sea towards the other end of the world, all its rivers and mountains stretching out below his feet, and at last a great ocean upon which no sail was spread. There, following the course given him to steer by the sun and the stars, he spied out the island whereon lived those hateful sisters, among lifeless images of men and beasts whom their looks had turned to stone.

Swooping down in the brightness of noonday, he saw the three Gorgons fast asleep, Medusa in the middle. But on her he did not dare to fix his eyes. As Athene had bidden him, he drew near with his back turned, holding her shield so as to make a mirror for that blood-curdling head, with its mane of vipers curling and writhing about it even in sleep. Fearfully beautiful was Medusa's face as well as horrible; but as she tossed to and fro in her dreams, Perseus saw how her body was clad in loathsome scales and brazen plumage, and how her limbs ended in cruel claws; and her mouth open in a bitter smile showed fangs like a serpent's, bristling round her forked tongue.

He durst not look longer for fear she should open her blood-freezing eyes. Marking in his mirror how she lay, he struck backwards, and with

The Doom Fulfilled by E. Burne-Jones, gouache, 151 × 137 cm, 1876–1885. (Southampton City Art Gallery, England.) "With one sweep of the crooked sword, he cut clean through her neck."

The Birth of Pegasus and Chrysaor from the Blood of Medusa (left), by E. Burne-Jones, gouache, 1876–1885. (Southampton City Art Gallery, England.)

one sweep of the crooked sword of Hermes had cut clean through her neck so swiftly as to choke her one shrill cry. Then with averted looks and shuddering hands he stowed away the bleeding head in his goatskin bag, and rose into the air with a shout of triumph.

That cry awoke the two sister Gorgons to find Medusa's headless body lying between them, and to hear the exulting voice of the foe who had done this deed. Hissing and howling, they spread their wings like monstrous birds of prey to seek him out with their iron talons. But Perseus, hid from them by his helm of darkness, was soon beyond reach of those revengeful monsters, that, unlike their sister, could not be slain by mortal hand.

Fast and far the hero flew with his prize, the way soon leading over a boundless desert on which he could see no green thing nor any living creature. But as the Gorgon's blood oozed through the goatskin, gouts of it dropped upon the thirsty sand, and there bred venomous snakes and scorpions, ever since to plague that barren soil. Huge pillars of whirling sand rose up to mark how the raging Gorgons chased him in vain; for Perseus soared above them invisible, nor set foot on earth till he came at evening to the westernmost bounds of the known world.

Here night and day knelt the old giant Atlas, holding up by pillars the weight of the sky. Of him Perseus, wearied by his long travel, begged leave to stay and rest in the famed garden of golden apples which Atlas kept jealously enclosed under guard of a dragon. But the churlish giant bid him begone.

"I am a son of Zeus, and I have done a deed to earn better welcome," pleaded Perseus.

"A son of Zeus is fated to rob my garden!" growled the giant, remembering an oracle of old, which was indeed to be fulfilled by another hero, Hercules.

"If so chary of what is thine, take thou a gift from me!" And with this Perseus drew forth the Gorgon's head to hold it full in the giant's face.

Not another word did Atlas speak. This hugest of Titans had in an instant been turned to a stony peak, his tall head white with snows, his beard stiff with ice, his rocky ribs bristling with forests. And so he stands to this day, a lifeless mountain bearing up the clouds.

The Gorgons and Medusa. "Hissing and howling, they spread their wings like monstrous birds of prey." Shoulder decoration of a Dinos, by the Gorgon painter, *c.* 600–580 B.C. (The Louvre, Paris.)

Andromeda

His face set to the east, Perseus held an airy way, feeling himself truly invincible, now that to the god-given talismans he had added the spell of Medusa's head, which even in death could appal the strongest foe. When he had passed over the desert, and crossed the green edges of the Nile, he came next to the land of the Ethiopians, and other strange peoples; and soon the rising sun showed him a marvellous sight. Against a black rock on the seashore, the form of a sunburnt maiden stood like a statue, nor moved as he swept down towards her, so that but for the tears in her eyes and her long locks stirred by the wind, he might have taken her for carved out of stone. He saw how, veiled in sunlight and spray, she blushed at his approach, faintly struggling as if she would have covered her face with her hands, but could not, for she was fast chained to the rock.

"Fair maiden, how comest thou in such a plight?" he cried, wondering at her beauty, not less than her woe.

"I am Andromeda, only daughter of Cepheus the king; and here am I set to suffer for words not my own. It was my mother Cassiope who, in her pride, boasted of me as fairer than the Nereids, daughters of the sea. They, out of spite, worked on Poseidon to send a cruel sea-monster, ravaging our coasts, and scaring the people from their homes. Then my father sought the oracle of Ammon in the Libyan sands, and had for answer that by the sacrifice of his daughter alone could the pest be stayed. So here I stand helpless, awaiting the monster, that is to devour me at sunrise, then leave the land in peace. And there he comes!" she ended with a shriek, as afar off rose a shapeless black bulk from the sea depths.

"Not helpless, fair Andromeda!" quoth Perseus, and with his magic sword cut the chains that bound her as lightly as if they were thread. "By heavenly aid, I have slain the Gorgon, and so will I do to this monster, be it ever so fearful."

Now the maiden stood still and calm, trusting that here must indeed be a son of the gods sent to deliver her. But her cry of alarm had come echoed back from the cliffs, on which stood the woeful parents with a crowd of people, waiting to see her cruel end. Their warning shouts told how that the monster made speed towards the victim, who closed her eyes when she saw its back cleaving the waves like a swift galley.

With one word of cheer to Andromeda, Perseus made ready for the fight that should deliver her. He laid aside Medusa's head, veiling its horror in seaweeds that afterwards were found changed into coral branches. Drawing his sword, he sprang lightly into the air, and flew to meet the monster as it rushed upon Andromeda with foaming jaws and grinding teeth. But when from above the hero's shadow fell upon the sea, the creature checked its course to rage against this unlooked-for enemy. Down swooped Perseus like an eagle, piercing its scaly neck with his keen blade. The monster roared and lashed and writhed, turning on its back as it vainly tried to get him into its horrid jaws, while again and again the sword goaded it to fresh fury upon the waves purpled with its blood; and to those looking on with affrighted eyes it seemed as if the whole sea were stirred by a storm.

At last, when all was still, the weeping parents ventured down from the cliff to see what had befallen. They found their daughter trembling but unharmed, and beside her Perseus stood wiping his sword, where out of the heaving red water stood up the monster's body, now still as a huge black reef.

"Dry your tears and take back your daughter, loosed by my sword," was the greeting of Perseus. "But her whom I have won from death, I claim

Pallas–Athene, 107 cm high. Second-century A.D. copy of the statue by Phidias which once stood in the Parthenon. (National Museum, Athens.) Athene bears on her breast-plate the Gorgon's head which even in death could appal the strongest foe.

for a kinder embrace. I am the son of Zeus and Danaë, one whom ye might not despise for her husband, even were she free to choose."

The grateful parents willingly agreed to give such a champion not only their daughter, but all the kingdom if he desired it as dowry. With tears, now of joy, they led him to their palace, where a feast was soon prepared to grace the marriage of Perseus and Andromeda, more lovely than ever in her bridal array.

But their wedding feast was troubled by a clang of arms, when into the hall burst Phineus, kinsman of the king, by whom the maid had before been sought in marriage. Backed by a throng of armed henchmen, he demanded his promised bride, hotly defying the favoured lover.

"No stranger is worthy to win the daughter of our land!" he declared; and not a few of the guests cried out on his side.

"Thou didst not woo her when chained to the rock!" taunted Perseus. "Neither suitor nor kinsman stood by her against the monster from whose jaws I won Andromeda to be mine."

For answer Phineus hurled his spear, that stuck quivering in a post beside Perseus as he stood with his shield held over Andromeda. His sword flashed out like lightning, and in a moment the hall was filled with uproar. Song and mirth gave place to the clash and hiss of weapons, and the tables ran red with blood instead of wine. So many were the followers and well-wishers of Phineus that the king's men could not withstand them; then over the din rose the hero's voice:

"Let all who are my friends turn away their eyes!"

He held up the Gorgon's head, and in the twinkling of an eye those enemies had been turned to stone as they stood, one brandishing a sword, one flinging a dart, and Phineus, last of all, upon his knees as he fell to beg for his own life when he saw what befell his comrades in rebellion. Not thus could they now disturb the marriage banquet.

The Minister of Doom

Men say that the rock from which Perseus loosed Andromeda may still be seen at Joppa below Jerusalem. However that may be, in the kingdom of Cepheus he built a ship, on which to carry home his bride to Seriphos. He reached the island to hear heartstirring news. His mother was still alive, but Polydectes had made her a slave, ever persecuting her with his hateful love, so that she had been driven to take sanctuary from him in Athene's temple. Spurred by wrath, Perseus strode to the hall of that tyrant, and found him revelling among his drunken companions.

"Ha, foundling, whom we never thought to see again!" was his scornful welcome. "Hast brought the Gorgon's head?"

"Behold!" said Perseus sternly, as he uncovered the blood-curdling trophy, before which those mockers were forthwith turned to stone; and there they stand in a ring, washed evermore by wind and weather.

In place of Polydectes, Danaë's son made the good Dictys chief of the

Head of Medusa. "So hideous that those who set eyes on her turned to stone". Clay tablet from the Temple of Apollo, 7th century B.C. (Villa Giuglia, Rome.)

Perseus Turns Polydectes to Stone. "Hast brought the Gorgon's head?" scorned Polydectes. "Behold!" said Perseus. Engraving from an illustrated edition of *Metamorphoses* by Ovid. Published in 1683 in Amsterdam.

Perseus Rescuing Andromeda, by Joachim Wtewael, 1566–1638. (The Louvre, Paris.) "Down swooped Perseus, like an eagle."

island. Now, from his joyful mother he learned how he was grandson of the king of Argos, and set out forthwith to claim his rightful heritage. But first he piously restored the magic gifts of the gods; and to Athene he gave the head of that Gorgon foe of gods and men, to be set as a boss in her dazzling shield, and serve her as the dread Ægis thrown over the innocent in the eyes of those who would do them wrong.

Acrisius had heard with dread of his grandson being still alive and on his way to Argos. Always bearing in mind the words of the oracle that he should die by this hand, he waited not his coming, but fled to Larissa in the land of the Thessalians. Thither Perseus followed, hoping to persuade his grandfather that he meant him no harm. He came to Larissa when its king was holding games, at which old Acrisius sat among the onlookers. The young stranger joined in these sports, and all wondered how easily he bore off the prize in racing and wrestling. But when his name ran from lip to lip, Acisius shrank into the shade and covered his face, fearing to be known by that fated offspring.

It came to throwing the quoit, and again Perseus hurled far beyond all

Atlas Turned to Stone, by E. Burne-Jones, gouache, 150 × 190 cm, 1876–1885. (Southampton City Art Gallery, England.) The huge Titan was in an instant turned to a stony peak.

25

his competitors. But there rose a sudden gust of wind that carried his strongest cast aside, so that the quoit struck Acrisius; and such a hurt was enough to end his old and feeble life. Perseus stood horror-struck to learn how by chance he had been the death of his own grandsire. After burying the body and purifying himself by due rites from his unconscious guilt, he went back to Argos, but could not with a quiet mind keep the inheritance thus won. He exchanged his kingdom with the neighbour king of Tiryns, and built for himself the great city Mycenæ.

Many famous heroes sprang from one whom men came to look on as half-divine; and after their death, Perseus and Andromeda, with Cepheus and Cassiope, were placed by the gods among the bright stars that guide wandering mariners.

MELEAGER AND ATALANTA
The Boar Hunt

In Calydon, fair country of Ætolia, to King Oineus and his wife Althæa was born a son whom they named Meleager. And when the babe was not a week old, there came to the house three lame and wrinkled old women,

Meleager, from *Manual of Mythology* by A.S. Murray, 1873, London. Meleager was destined to live only so long as the firebrand burning at his birth remained unconsumed.

The Calydonian Boar Hunt (right). "A monstrous boar with glaring eyes and foaming jaws, its bristles like sword points, its tusks like those of an elephant." Sarcophagus relief, first to second century A.D. (Woburn Abbey, Bedfordshire, England.)

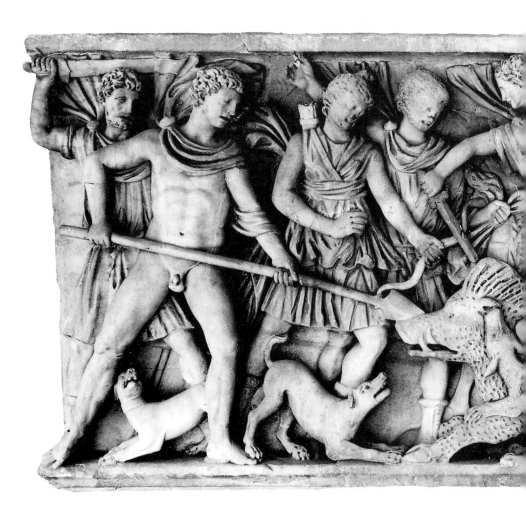

busy night and day with their distaffs, spinning the thread of men's life. For these were no other than the Fates, who, as they bent over the newborn child, croned out his fortune thus:–

"He will grow a goodly man, like his father," quoth the first.

"He will be a hero renowned through the world," murmured the second.

"He will live," murmured the third, "only so long as that firebrand on the hearth remains unconsumed."

The anxious mother's ear caught those words; then no sooner had the weird sisters vanished, than she rose from her bed to seize the firebrand, quench it in water, and hide it away among her most secret treasures.

Young Meleager grew up, as had been foretold, a son to be the pride of any mother. He made one of the band of heroes who went with Jason to seek the Golden Fleece; and when they came home, another feat of arms awaited him to celebrate his name by the slaying of the Calydonian boar.

In his son's absence, King Oineus had drawn upon himself the wrath of a goddess. As thanksgiving for a fruitful year, he loaded the altar of Demeter with corn, to Dionysus he poured out wine, and to Athene oil; but he forgot any sacrifice to Artemis, and that haughty maiden avenged herself on the mortal who had failed in doing her honour. She sent into his country a monstrous boar with glowing eyes and foaming jaws, its bristles

Diana (Artemis), by Auguste Renoir, canvas, 199.5 × 129.5 cm, 1867. (National Gallery of Art, Washington.) Twin-sister to Apollo, Artemis was the chaste and maiden goddess of the moon, the hunt and the woods. Oineus unwittingly invoked the wrath of the goddess in failing to honour her.

strong and sharp like sword points, its tusks long as those of an elephant, its breath so fiery as to scare man and beast when it broke crashing through the woods. Wherever it ravaged, the crops were trampled down, the herds scattered at its onset, the shepherds fled from their flocks, and the husbandmen durst not venture out to pluck the fruit of their vines and olives, left to hang rotting on the trees.

So when Meleager came home from Colchis, it was to find his father's land laid waste by the fear of this monster. At once he set about gathering hunters and hounds to track it to its lair, as no man had yet dared to do. He was readily joined by several of his fellow venturers on the Argo, not yet tired of perilous quests; and in all Greece could be seen no such gallant band as now joined together to hunt down the Calydonian boar.

Among the rest came the maiden huntress, Atalanta, of whom strange tales were told. Her father, too, was a king, and had hoped for a son like Meleager to be his heir; so, when a daughter was born to him, in his anger he threw her out to die upon a wild mountain. But there the child, men say, was suckled by a she-bear, then in its den found by hunters, who brought her up to their own rude life. Thus she grew man-like and hardy, careless of wind or weather, not less bold than beautiful, skilled to handle bow and spear, and more willing to face the fiercest beast than to listen to tender words. All her heart was set on hunting and strenuous exercises, and she thought of men only as comrades in sports, at which few youths could surpass her by strength or courage. More than one, rashly seeking to woo her, had rough handling to take for his answer.

"Happy the man who can find such a mate," was Meleager's first thought when he saw Atalanta, with her brown face like a lad's, her hair loosely tied back upon her broad shoulders, bearing a spear as lightly as if it were a spindle, and carrying bow and quiver slung about her sturdy sun-tanned limbs. But others murmured that their quest was none for women; and grudges rose against this unknown companion, who only asked a chance to prove her prowess. It was no time, indeed, for wooing nor for quarrelling, so without delay the whole band set forth to seek their fearsome quarry.

No hard task was theirs to find the boar, that soon came raging through the forest to meet those champions. The nets were spread to catch it; the hounds were turned into the thorny thickets; but the monster needed no rousing. Out of a bed of reeds it broke upon them, a grisly sight that set the dogs turning tail, when their masters stood fast to hurl a cloud of darts, and the first spear-point that drew blood was Atalanta's.

Maddened by wounds, with heaving sides and gnashing jaws, the boar dashed among them like a thunderbolt, laying low three or four with its dripping tusks before they could fetch a blow. One was fain to save himself by swinging up into the boughs of an oak, on the trunk of which the horrid foe sharpened its deadly tusks in vain, till a rash hound came within reach to be tossed howling into the air. One dog after another, too, was hurt by their own masters, as the spears flew amiss. Running on with

Frontispiece to an illustrated edition of *Metamorphoses*, the best-known work of the Roman poet, Ovid, 43 B.C. to 17 A.D. Published in 1683 in Amsterdam.

Landscape with Meleager and Atalanta, by Gian Battista Viola, oil on panel, 99 × 77 cm, *c.* 1613. "Happy the man who can find such a mate", Meleager thought when he first saw Atalanta.

axe heaved above his head, one bold hunter slipped upon the grass wet with blood and lay a helpless victim in the monster's way. But when the man gave ground before its charge, Atalanta's arrow flew with so true an aim that the bristling boar again stopped short to rage out its pain.

"Verily, maiden, thou art the best man of us all!" cried Meleager; and the rest of the hunters, ashamed to be outdone by a woman, once more closed to the attack.

A score of wounds in turn brought the monster to the ground; and when it got to its feet it was to stagger and turn round and round, blinded by blood. Red froth poured out of its jaws, choking its angry growls; its fiery eyes grew dim; and when at length Meleager thrust his sword to the hilt in its reeking sides, the huge beast lay writhing in its own gore mingled with that of its conquerors, never more to be a terror to the land.

The boar's death-throes were hardly at an end before Meleager planted his foot on its neck with a shout of exultation. Making haste to cut off the bleeding head and to strip away the bristly skin, he offered these trophies to Atalanta as the one that of all had best deserved them, though they fell to himself whose fortune was to give the fatal stroke. But against this some of the hunters cried out in displeasure, loudest of all the two Thestiades, brothers of Althæa and uncles to Meleager.

"This is no woman's work, nor is its prize for a maiden!" clamoured the jealous men; and those sons of Thestios made bold to tear the spoils from Atalanta's hands.

Thus began a brawl in which the heroes turned on one another, their weapons still warm from the boar's blood. So hot waxed the quarrel, that Meleager in his own defence shed the life blood of both those kinsmen, who would have scorned the fair huntress. So all their jubilation was changed to bitterness and grief for friends slain over the body of their foe.

Althaea Removes the Firebrand from the Fire, to save her son from his fate. From an illuminated copy of *Metamorphoses* by Ovid, late fifteenth century.

An ill day was that for the house of Oineus, on which its brave son made an end of the boar. When the news came to Althæa, she had gone out to the temple to give proud thanks, but on the way fell in with a mourning train that bore her dearly loved brothers to their funeral pyre. Too soon she learned by whose hand they had fallen; then, beside herself for sorrow, she was moved to curse her own son. Beating her breast and tearing her hair with wild outcry, she broke open the secret place in which she kept hidden away that quenched firebrand that measured his days of life. Furiously she ran with it to where the sacrificial fire burned on the altar. In her madness she scarce knew what she did, yet thrice, four times, she drew back from her unnatural purpose, the mother and the sister warring in her breast. But as her eyes fell on the blood-stained corpses of her own mother's sons, with shuddering hand and averted face she hurled that brand upon the flame. Quickly was it burned to ashes; then as quickly her rage melted to heartbreaking repentance. When soon she heard what came of her vengeful frenzy, the woebegone mother saw nothing for it but to end her own days, dying with her brethren, beside the embers on which she had quenched the life of her son.

For as Meleager came bringing home in triumph the spoils of the great hunt, suddenly his steps had faltered and his eyes grew dim as if blinded by the smoke of that consuming firebrand. A hot fever filled his veins, while his heart dried up and his spirit withered away as a dead leaf. With a groan of amazement he fell like the trunk of some thunder-stricken oak, to breathe his last without a wound, nor ever knew how he had come to so untimely death. And thus was accomplished the decree of those fatal sisters that looked upon his birth.

Atalanta's Race

When the boar of Calydon had been quelled by Meleager's doughty band, Atalanta would have gone back to her savage haunts, caring not to consort with men since he was dead who alone had stirred her heart. But that feat had come to the ears of her harsh sire Iasos, who might well be moved to pride in such a daughter. He sought her out and brought her home to his kingdom, still without an heir.

Atalanta's Race, from an illuminated copy of *Metamorphoses* by Ovid, late fifteenth century. Atalanta muses over the golden apples.

Many were the suitors willing to win a bride so fair and so famous, daughter of a sonless king, and well able to hold her own in arms. But Atalanta would have none of them, choosing to remain a virgin, like the goddess of hunting to whom she was vowed. Still she practised many exercises, scorning all softness, and having no skill in women's work. When her father pressed her to wed, she made one and another excuse; then at last agreed to take the wooer who could outstrip her in running; but death to be his lot if he failed to win the race.

Even on such hard conditions, brave and agile youths came forward to run for their lives against Atalanta's hand. She, fleet as a fawn, lightly outran the swiftest footed; and one after another they paid their rashness by a cruel end, for, while the suitor must run naked and unarmed, the fierce maiden bore a spear, with which she goaded them not to victory but to death. Still, the sight of their heads set up as a warning by the goal did not chill the hearts of other adventurers, hoping to win the prize where so many had shamefully failed. Among the rest was young Hippomenes, who, while acting as judge at such a contest, had let his own heart be inflamed by Atalanta's scornful eyes.

Before he offered himself to the trial, not trusting wholly in his breath and sinews, like the rest, Hippomenes had implored the favour of Aphrodite on that strange course of love. And the goddess heard and helped him with a gift, that by her counsel should serve him well. Three golden apples she gave him to carry in his hands as he ran, and what he was to do with them came from her knowing the heart of woman better than was open to man's wit.

Away went youth and maiden, racing towards the goal. Before long Atalanta was like to pass her competitor, who then slyly threw down one of the golden apples to roll across her way. Tempted by wonder or curiosity, she stooped to pick it up, while Hippomenes pressed swiftly on.

After brief delay it was easy for her to catch up with him, but now he threw away the second apple, and again she halted to seize it. Again she followed hot-foot, when he, panting towards the goal, let the third apple fall before her. And lo! while once more she tarried to gain that glittering prize, her wily suitor had won the race.

Thus taken in her own snare, the manlike maiden could not but give her hand to Hippomenes, who hoped to win her heart withal. But he, poor youth, had short joy in his fortune. For, as Oineus neglected to propitiate Artemis, so this exultant bridegroom forgot to give thanks to Aphrodite for her favouring aid. Thereon the resentful goddess no longer smiled but frowned upon their love. She led them into offence against Rhea, mighty mother of the gods, who transformed that bold runner and his ungentle bride into a pair of lions, harnessed to her car when she drove forth amid a wild din of horns and cymbals.

HERCULES
His Youth

Hercules, whom the Greeks called Herakles, was the strongest man on earth, being indeed of the blood of the gods. Amphitryon, king of Tiryns, passed for his father, who had married Alcmene, granddaughter of Perseus; but his true sire was Zeus himself, who had deceived this queen in the form of her husband. When his birth was at hand, the ruler of Olympus proclaimed that the child born that day should be lord over all Greece. Then Hera, in hatred of her secret stepson, brought about that his birth was hindered, and that his cousin Eurystheus came into the world before him, whereby afterwards Hercules was doomed to serve that unworthy kinsman.

Alcmene so well guessed how the jealous mistress of heaven would plot against her son, that she durst not nurse him at home, but had him exposed in a field, trusting that Zeus would not fail to protect his own offspring. There, then, came by Hera and Athene, wondering at this sight of a naked, new-born child. Hera, unaware who it was, caught up the babe to hold it to her breast, but it sucked so violently that she threw it down in anger. Athene, more patient and pitiful, carried the unknown Hercules to the city, and gave him to his own mother to be brought up as a foundling.

Joyfully Alcmene undertook to rear her child, hoping that the few drops of Hera's milk he had sucked would save him from the goddess's ill-will. But when Hera came to know who was the babe she had saved from death, her heart was hot with spite. She sent two snakes to kill him in his cradle. While his mother slept, those ministers of her vengeance had twisted themselves about the child's neck. The nurse sitting by could not move nor speak for horror. But Hercules awoke with a shout that roused his anxious mother to see how her lusty babe had caught one snake in

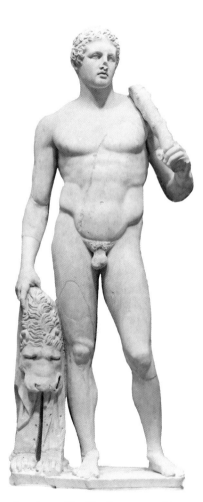

Lansdowne Herakles, Roman, marble. 1.935 m. high, *c.* A.D. 135. (J. Paul Getty Museum, Malibu, California.) Hercules, known by the Romans as Herakles, was "the strongest man on earth."

The Infant Hercules Strangling Snakes (opposite). "Her lusty babe caught one snake in each hand and laughingly strangled them before they could do him harm." Fresco from the House of the Vetii, Pompeii.

*The Choice of Hercules Between
Pleasure and Virtue* by David Ligare.
Oil on canvas, 198 × 246 cm, 1986.
(Koplin Gallery, Los Angeles.)
"Pleasure, loved by most men . . . or
Duty, whom few learn to love?"

each hand, and laughingly strangled them before they could do him harm. Alcmene's cries in turn brought in her husband with drawn sword, who might well stand amazed at such a feat of infant strength. He sent for Tiresias to cast the child's fortune; and that blind seer now let him know the origin and destiny of Hercules.

Henceforth Amphitryon spared no pains on the bringing up of so wonderful a foster-son. He himself taught the boy to tame horses and to drive a chariot. The most famous teachers of arts and exercises were sought out for him all over Greece, among them Linus, son of Apollo, to be his master in music. But when Linus one day would have chastised this sturdy pupil, Hercules smote him to death with one blow of the lute, thus early indulging the hot temper that was to cost him dear. After this Amphitryon sent him from home to dwell among his herdsmen on the mountains, where he grew taller and stronger than any man in Greece, able to fell an ox with his fist, and never missing his aim with the bow or the spear. He is also said to have made one of that fellowship of young heroes who were schooled in the cave of the wise Centaur Cheiron.

Hercules Wrestling with the Nemean Lion, Psiax. "He cast his arms round its neck, and choked it to death." Obverse of amphora, 58.5 cm high, *c.* 520 B.C., Vulci. (Museo Civico de Brescia, Italy.)

There came a time when the full-growth youth must choose whether his strength should be turned to good or evil. Wandering alone, he met two beautiful women, each beckoning him to follow her on a different path. She who spoke first was full-fed and richly arrayed.

"My name," spoke she, "is Pleasure, loved by the most of men. See how my path is broad and easy and soft to the feet! Take this way and thou shalt never want rich food and drink, nor fine raiment and soft beds, nor any cheer of life, and all without pain or peril. Come, then, with me!"

The youth looked willingly at this fair temptress, yet before taking her hand, he turned to the other, who pointed out an opposite way. She appeared more modest and maidenly, clad in simple white without gauds or jewels, and in a low voice she spoke thus:–

"My name is Duty, whom no man dares to scorn, yet few learn to love. My path indeed will prove steep and thorny, and on it I promise not ease and pleasure, but labour and smarting. Yet pain bravely borne shall turn to joy and pride. So shall he who follows me win honour and peace upon earth, and at last his birthright among the gods."

For a moment the hero stood in doubt, then his swelling heart went out to Duty, and he gave her his hand. Thus was made the Choice of Hercules, whose sorest sufferings would come when he strayed from that toilsome path.

His Labours

Having chosen Duty as his guide, Hercules followed her to become the most famous champion of his age. He slew cruel giants, he exterminated fierce wild beasts; everywhere he hastened to help the oppressed. Gods as well as men hailed his mighty deeds. Athene equipped him in armour from her own temple; Hermes gave him a resistless sword; Apollo furnished him with sharp arrows; and he bore a famous pictured shield, the work of Hephæstus at the bidding of Zeus. Thus arrayed, he flew to the aid of Thebes when it was threatened by an invader haughtily demanding tribute. This city, indeed, was dear to Hercules, since his reputed father Amphitryon, his own kingdom given up, had made his home there. In the battle for its defence Amphitryon fell; but the prowess of his son gained the victory. The grateful Creon, king of Thebes, gave Hercules his daughter Megara in marriage; and it seemed as if he had no more to wish for on earth.

But nothing could make Hera forget her hatred to this son of Zeus. She sent upon the hero a furious madness, in which he threw his own children upon a fire and drove his wife from him in horror. When his frenzy passed away, letting him know what he had done, he fell into deep melancholy, and for a time was seen no more among men, while he sought pardon and healing from the gods. As penance it was appointed him to become vassal to his kinsman Eurystheus, he who, by Hera's cunning trick, had gained the birthright promised by Zeus. Humbly Hercules stooped his pride to serve that poor-spirited and faint-hearted lord, spending now the best years of his manhood in labours beyond the power of any but himself. On ten weary errands must he go at the bidding of Eurystheus, before he could be his own man again: such was the decree given forth from the oracle at Delphi.

The first task set him was to slay the Nemean lion, a savage monster that had long kept the land of Argolis in dread. Armed only with his bow, and with a wild olive tree he tore up by the roots to make him a club, Hercules hunted through the forest of Nemea where the lion had its lair. Before long its fearsome roar led him to a thicket, from which it burst towards him open-mouthed. Hercules drew his bow with true aim, but one and another arrow fell harmless from the creature's hide. But with his club the hero laid it low in the act to spring; then, flinging away his weapons, he threw himself upon the writhing beast, cast his arms round its neck, and choked it to death. When he had flayed it with its own sharp claws, he hung the skin about him as a garment and helmed himself with its head. By these spoils and by his huge club, this lion-killer was henceforth known wherever he went.

The second task laid upon Hercules was to quell a monster haunting the marshes of Lerna. This was the Hydra, that huge snake with nine heads, one of which could not be hurt by any weapon, and the others would grow again as fast as they were cut off. Accompanied by his nephew Iolaus, the hero set out for Lerna in a swift chariot, and soon found the wooded hill where the Hydra kept itself hidden. Leaving his nephew beside the horses, with fiery arrows he fetched the creature from out of its hole, to swoop upon him, hissing and spitting from all its heads, that waved like branches in a storm. Undismayed, Hercules met its onset and mowed down the twisting heads one by one, yet as fast as he cut them off two grew up in place of one, while it twined its loathsome body round

Hercules Slays the Hydra of Lerna. Caeretan, *c.* 525 B.C. (J. Paul Getty Museum, Malibu, California.) The hydra was a huge nine-headed snake which ravaged the country of Lerna.

Hercules and the Erymanthian Boar, by the Lysippides painter. Attic black figure oinochoe, *c.* 530 B.C., from Vulci. (The British Museum, London.) "Hercules wearied it out with chasing it in deep snowdrifts."

Hercules and the Stymphalian Birds. "As the birds rose in the air, he shot them with his deadly arrows." Attic black figure amphora, *c.* 550 B.C., from Vulci. (The British Museum, London.)

his limbs and almost stifled him with its foul breath. He was fain to call for the help of Iolaus, who ran up with a torch; then as Hercules shore off the bristling heads, his nephew seared each bleeding wound, so that they could not grow again. At last the raging Hydra was left with that one head no iron could wound; but Hercules crushed it with his club, and tore it off and buried it in the ground under a heavy rock. In its poisonous blood the conqueror dipped his arrows, to make the hurt from them henceforth incurable.

His third labour was to bring in alive the golden-antlered and brazen-hoofed stag Cerynitis, that roamed free upon the Arcadian hills. A bold man he would have been who should slay that beast, sacred as it was to Artemis. For a year Hercules chased it in its native haunts and far beyond; it led him out of Greece to Thrace; and on over barbarous wildernesses, and deep into the northern darkness. Foiled again and again, he had nothing for it but to lame the agile stag with a dart, then he could catch it to bear home on his shoulders. By the way he fell in with Artemis, wroth against him for hurting a beast under her protection. But a hero can soothe even an offended goddess; and she let him carry the stag to Eurystheus.

The fourth labour was to catch a grimmer beast, that boar that ravaged the Erymanthian mountain ridge between Attica and Elis. On his way to this adventure, Hercules brought on a strange battle, against his will. He was entertained by a Centaur named Pholus, who set before him meat enough but no wine, for he had only one cask, the gift of Dionysus, which belonged to the Centaurs in common, and must not be opened unless all the race were there to share it. Yet Hercules persuaded his host to broach that cask; and when the fumes of strong wine spread through the woods, the other Centaurs came trampling up, armed with rocks and fir branches. In their anger over the broached cask, they would have fallen upon the stranger, who stoutly defended himself, and his invincible arrows drove them to take shelter in the cave of Cheiron, his old teacher. That good Centaur, in the fray, was hurt by a chance arrow, which, dipped in the Hydra's poisonous blood, killed him in slow agony, all his own arts of healing being in vain. Pholus, too, the kindly host, died from handling one of those deadly arrows, which he let fall on his foot. Having mournfully done the last offices to those friends on whom he had brought such suffering, Hercules held on to the haunts of the Erymanthian boar, which he drove from the forests up to the bare crests, and wearied it out with chasing in deep snowdrifts till he could bind it with cords to bring alive to Eurystheus.

His fifth labour was cleansing in a single day the stables of Augeas, king of Elis, who kept three thousand cattle, but for thirty years had not taken the trouble to clear out the enclosures heaped with their filth. When he saw Hercules present himself for a task so unworthy of a hero, Augeas laughed, and lightly promised him one-tenth of his herds, if he would do the work that seemed beyond a giant's power. But Hercules was crafty as

well as stout. He saw how the rivers Peneus and Alpheus flowed hard by, whose waters he brought by a new channel to sweep through the Augean stables, and thus cleansed them out in a day. Now that Augeas heard how he came sent by Eurystheus for this very task, he was for refusing the promised reward; but Hercules held him to his offer, calling to witness against him his own son Phyleus, in whose presence it was made; and when Phyleus testified truly, the angry father drove him from home, along with the hero who had done him so good service. Years later, Hercules came back to teach that churlish lord how ill he had done in breaking his word with such a servant.

The sixth labour was hunting out the Stymphalides, those same arrow-feathered birds of prey that troubled the voyage of the Argonauts. Lake Stymphalis in Arcadia was their breeding place, which Hercules found black with such a throng of the mischievous fowl that he knew not how to deal with them. But Athene, goddess of invention, came to his aid, giving him a huge pair of brass clappers made by Hephæstus, to raise a rattle louder than all the screeching of the birds. Taking post on a hill, Hercules startled them up by the clappers, then, as they rose in the air, shot them down with his deadly arrows; and those that flew away were so scared as never again to be seen in Greece.

The seventh labour was to master a bull wandering madly about the

Hercules Slays the Centaurs, by Charles Le Brun, oil on canvas, 77.5 × 112 cm, *c.* 1660. "The centaurs came trampling up, armed with rocks and fir branches." (National Gallery of Canada, Ottawa.)

island of Crete. Minos, its king, willingly gave him leave to chase down this pest that worked havoc through his dominions, and no man had yet been able to tame it. But Hercules caught the bull, and mounted its back, and rode it through the sea to Greece. There Eurystheus turned it loose, again to be a terror to the people, till it was hunted down on the plain of Marathon by Theseus, him who ever took pride in doing deeds after the pattern of his great kinsman.

The eighth labour of Hercules was to catch the mares of Diomedes, a Thracian chief, who reared his horses to be savage as himself by feeding them on human flesh. The hero first took Diomedes captive and gave him as food to his own wild mares, which after devouring their master, let Hercules drive them away quietly as kids. Yet they were not wholly weaned from their fierce nature, as, while he made a stand against the Thracians pursuing him, the troop of mares tore in pieces his companion Abderus, set to guard them; and Hercules had to tame them afresh. Men say that a horse of this breed was that Bucephalus long afterwards mastered by Alexander of Macedon.

The ninth labour was to win for Eurystheus's daughter the girdle of Hippolyte, gift of Ares to that queen of the warlike Amazons, who lived far away in Asia. So un-womanlike were they as to kill all their male children; and they burned away their right breasts not to be hindered in the use of the bow. Hippolyte was so charmed by the looks and bearing of this foe that she offered to give up her girdle freely. But Hera, taking the form of an Amazon, stirred up the virago people against him, nor could her stepson bring off that trophy without a hard battle. As he carried it back to Greece, Hercules passed by Troy, and there saved the daughter of its king Laomedon from the claws of a monster, as Perseus freed Andromeda. This king, also, cheated the hero of his promised reward; then Hercules vowed to come back and leave no stone of Troy standing upon another, as he did in after-years.

The tenth labour for Eurystheus, that should have been the last, was to bring a herd of red cattle belonging to the giant Geryon, from the island Erythia by the western ocean, where they fed under guard of the two-headed dog Orthrus; and Geryon himself was so monstrous that he had three bodies, three heads, six arms, and six feet, being the son of Chrysaor, a giant engendered from the blood of Medusa, slain by Perseus. The more Hercules toiled for his kinsman, the more that cowardly king hated him, envying his prowess; and now Eurystheus hoped to be rid of him, sent so far against such a foe. But Hercules set out cheerful and undismayed, undertaking by the way exploits that would have appalled most men. Reaching the straits of Gades, he there set up two landmarks henceforth famed as the pillars of Hercules. Thirsty after long wandering through waterless deserts, the heat of the sun so irked him that he dared to point his arrows against Phœbus, lord of the sky. Yet noble Apollo took no offence at his boldness, but favoured him with a golden boat in which he passed over to Erythia, where he slew the three-headed giant and his

Hercules and Hippolyte, Queen of the Amazons. The Amazons were warlike females who killed their male children, but Hippolyte was charmed by Hercules. Book plate.

Diomedes Devoured by his Horses (opposite), by Gustave Moreau, oil on canvas, 138.5 × 84.5 cm, 1865. (Musée des Beaux Arts, Rouen, France.) "After devouring their master, they let Hercules drive them away as quietly as kids."

two-headed dog, nay, shot an arrow into the breast of Hera's self, who came to the aid of that monster against the man she ever hated.

Geryon's herd he then drove home over seas and rivers and mountains, yet not without fresh perils on the way. As he passed through Italy, the fire-breathing giant Cacus stole part of the cattle while their keeper lay asleep. To leave no plain trace of the theft, he dragged them into his cave backwards by the tail. Deceived by this trick, when he had searched all round, Hercules gave them up for lost; but as he drove the rest of the herd past that hidden cave, the beasts shut up within lowed back to their fellows. To seek them out was to put himself face to face with Cacus, who found too late how ill it was to rob such a stranger. Having slain the thievish giant, Hercules went on with the herd, and still had much ado to keep them together, for Hera sent a gadfly to drive them wild among the hills; and she flooded a water on his way, which he could not cross till he had filled up the channel with stones. It was then that he wandered far into the wilds of Scythia, and there dealt with another monster, half-woman, half-serpent. But in the end he brought the herd safe to Greece, to make for Eurystheus a rich sacrifice to that ungracious queen of heaven.

When now the hero hoped to be free, that mean-minded king still claimed his service. Two of the tasks he had accomplished Eurystheus refused to count among the ten: the slaying of the Hydra, because then Hercules had his nephew's help; and the cleansing of the Augean stables, because for that he had taken hire. So he must undertake two more labours, making twelve in all; and the last were the worst.

He was next sent to pluck three golden apples from a garden given by Gaia, the earth-mother, to Zeus and Hera on their marriage. The Garden of the Hesperides it was called, from those four nymphs, daughters of Night, who kept it; and for warder it had a sleepless hundred-headed dragon. No man even knew where this garden lay; and Hercules, in search of it, had to wander far and wide, everywhere slaying giants and monsters with his mighty club, nay once he came to blows with Ares himself, but Zeus by a thunderbolt parted those kinsmen of Olympian blood. At last the friendly nymphs of the Eridanus counselled the hero to ask his way from Nereus, Old Man of the Sea, who knew all things. So Hercules did, coming upon Nereus while he slept clad in dripping seaweeds, to bind him and hold fast his slippery body for all the changing forms it was his way to take, till, weary of the struggle, he told how to find the island Garden of the Hesperides in the western ocean.

Further directions he should get from Prometheus, who now for thirty years had been chained to an icy crag of the Caucasus, exposed by turns to scorching sun and freezing winds, while daily tormented by the talons of an eagle, or as some say, a vulture, the minister of Zeus. As Hercules strode across those giant mountains, he saw this bird flying on its cruel errand, and shot it with one of his fatal arrows. Thus guided to the place of punishment that should last for ages, it was easy for the hero to tear Prometheus loose; nor did Zeus resent that boldness of his son, but laid

Hercules Punishes Cacus for Stealing the Sacred Cattle. Engraving by C. David, after F. Floris, 1635.

The Torture of Prometheus (opposite), by Jean-Louis Cesar Lair, 1781–1828. (Musée Crozatier, Le Puy en Velay, France.) To punish Prometheus for stealing Fire, Zeus chained him to a mountain, where he was tormented by an eagle until Hercules delivered him.

The Garden of the Hesperides, by E. Burne-Jones, 1870–1877. (Private collection.) The garden was tended by four nymphs – Daughters of Night – and a sleepless, hundred-headed dragon.

aside his ire against the friend of man. The grateful prisoner, wise with age and lonely sorrow, repaid his release by good counsels for Hercules, bidding to seek out Atlas and ask him to fetch the golden apples from the Hesperides, who were thought to be his children.

So the messenger of Eurystheus held on to Africa, and first he came to Egypt, where the king, Busiris, had harsh welcome for strangers. Years before, a famine falling on his land, a certain soothsayer from Cyprus told how the gods' anger might be turned away by yearly sacrifice of some man not born on the soil. Busiris made this soothsayer his first sacrifice; and every year some stranger was marked for death. So Hercules, taken as a goodly victim, was brought to the sacrifice with laughter in his heart, for he burst the bonds like thread, killed the king at his own altar, and went his way from among the terrified Egyptians.

In Africa he overcame a doughtier foe, the giant Antæus, who challenged all-comers to wrestle with him for life or death, and could vanquish most men by the fresh strength it was his nature to draw in as often as he touched his mother-earth. But the hero had craft as well as strength to hold Antæus up in the air and there choke the breath out of him, so that he troubled travellers no more. Hercules also cleared the Libyan sands of wild beasts, as was his wont wherever he came.

So, after long travel, he found Atlas, where that weary giant bears up the weight of the world. Hercules offered to take the burden for a time on his own shoulders if Atlas would go for the golden apples, as he consented to do. But when he came back with three apples robbed from the garden, Atlas was unwilling to shoulder his heavy load again, now that he had felt what it was to stretch his limbs freely. The hero had to use cunning when force would not serve him. Feigning to be content, he only asked Atlas to hold the world for a little, while he wound cords about his own aching head to ease the pressure. The dull-witted giant did so; but no sooner had he the world on his back again, than Hercules made off with the golden apples, leaving Atlas taken by his own trick.

When once more he came back safe and successful, his unkind kinsman saw with despair how from all the perilous labours laid upon him Hercules but won more glory and goodwill as a benefactor of men. To make an end of him, Eurystheus chose a task that seemed beyond the might of any mortal; he sent his ever-victorious champion to fetch from the nether world Cerberus, the three-headed hound of hell. For this enterprise, Hercules piously prepared himself by visiting Eleusis, there being initiated into its mysteries and cleansed from the guilt of the Centaurs' blood. He then went to Tænarum, the southernmost point of the Peloponnesus, where a dark cave opened as one of the gates of Hades. The god Hermes led him below into that chill under-world, where the thin shades fled in affright from a being of flesh and blood; but Medusa stood to face him, and he would have drawn his sword upon her, had not

Hercules Aids Atlas to Support the World. Engraving by C. David, after F. Floris, 1635. Hercules took the world on his shoulders for a time, while Atlas stole the golden apples.

Hermes held his hand, bidding him remember how ghosts could no more be hurt by iron. The shade of Meleager, too, ventured up to whisper to him a message of love for his mourning sister Deianira, of which more was to come than he knew.

Near the gates of Hades, Hercules was amazed to find two living men chained to the black rock, and still more when he recognized them as his old comrades Theseus and Peirithous. For Peirithous, king of the Lapithæ, who fought their great battle with the Centaurs, had been so exalted with pride that he ventured to woo Persephone in hell itself, and his dear friend Theseus accompanied him on the too daring errand; then, seized by Pluto, they were both condemned to endless prison among the dead. Hope shone in their eyes at the sight of Hercules; pitiably they cried to him for

Hercules and the Brazen-hoofed Stag, Cerynitis. Hercules chased Cerynitis for a year, out of Greece into Thrace and beyond. Attic black figure amphora, *c.* 540 B.C., from Vulci. (The British Museum, London.)

Episodes from the Labours of Hercules: killing the hydra; mastering the Cretan bull; Hercules and Antaeus; the killing of Nessus . . . From an illustrated edition of *Metamorphoses* by Ovid, published in 1683 in Amsterdam.

help, which he did not grudge. He caught Theseus by the hand to tear him loose from his chains; and the king of Athens could thus win back for a time to the upper world. But when the hero would have freed Peirithous also, the rocks shook as from an earthquake, and he must leave that presumptuous man fast bound to his fate.

Yet so bold was he that he slew a bull of Pluto's cattle, pouring the blood into a trench for the wan ghosts to get a taste of life; and when the herdsman would have hindered, Hercules crushed his ribs, hardly letting him go but at the entreaty of his mistress Persephone. In such manner the hero stormed through hell till he came at last face to face with its dark-browed king, who barred his further passage. The undaunted one shot an arrow into Pluto's shoulder, making him roar for pain never felt before. Thus aware that this was an asker not to be denied, on learning his errand grim Pluto gave him leave to carry away Cerberus, if he could master it with his hands alone, using no weapon. Then at the mouth of Acheron, Hercules gripped that hellish watchdog by the throat, and, for all the terror of its three barking heads, its poison-dripping teeth, and its stinging tail like a scorpion's, he swung the loathly monster over his back and brought it up to earth to cast before the feet of Eruystheus.

This king, aghast at the very sight, could do nothing with Cerberus but let it go. As for Hercules, triumphant in every ordeal, Eurystheus gave up in despair his mastership over such a hero, and set him free on condition that he put back the monster at its fearsome watch post.

His Death

Thus released from his long servitude, Hercules still wandered about the world doing mighty deeds of strength to aid his fellow men. Yet ever Hera's ill will followed him, clouding his mind, so that here and there he turned aside from the chosen path of virtue. Athene for her part stood by him with help and counsel; and Zeus looked kindly upon the feats of his son, nor did he spare to chastise his spiteful queen when she took on her to send storms upon the hero's course. How he sailed with the Argonauts, how he dealt with the false king of Troy, how he brought back Alcestis to the house of Admetus, are famous tales often told.

Long ago, he had parted from his wife Megara, when he madly slew her children; and in time he sought another bride, Iole, daughter of King Eurytus, who in his youth had taught him the use of the bow. This renowned archer offered his daughter's hand as prize to whoever could shoot better than himself and his three sons. Hercules came to the trial and beat his old master. But when he claimed Iole, Eurytus was unwilling to let her marry a man known to have brought such woe on Megara. Among the king's sons, Iphitus alone took the part of him whom he loved and admired beyond all men; then, his bride being denied him Hercules went away in wrath.

Forthwith it chanced that certain oxen of Eurytus were stolen by the

Hercules and Antaeus. Son of Poseidon and Gē, Antaeus was a mighty giant whose strength was invincible so long as he remained in contact with his mother earth. Hercules discovered the giant's secret, lifted him from the earth, and crushed him in the air. Limoges plaque, grisaille, second half of the sixteenth century.

Hercules and Cerberus. Cerberus was the three-headed hound of Hell which guarded the entrance to the underworld. Hercules dragged him to the upper world. Limoges plaque, grisaille, second half of the sixteenth century.

noted thief Autolycus. The king made such of this as done by Hercules in revenge; but Iphitus would not believe such villainy of his friend. He sought out Hercules, and they joined together to hunt down the true robber. On their chase they had mounted a tower to look out for the stolen herd, when the hero's old madness returned upon him, and taking Iphitus as to blame for the ill will of his father, he hurled him from the tower in sudden fury.

When he came to himself and found that he had killed his best friend, Hercules passed into melancholy remorse. He pilgrimaged from one shrine to another, seeking to be purified from that sin. The oracle at Delphi at first refused to answer so blood-stained a suppliant; whereupon he threatened to rob the temple, to carry off the tripod and to set up an oracle of his own; then Zeus had some ado to make peace between his fierce son and the offended Apollo. In the end Hercules wrung from this god's priestess a sentence that his guilt could be purged away only by selling himself as a slave for three years, and giving the price to the children of Iphitus.

Willingly the hero stooped to this penance. In charge of Hermes, taking ship for Asia, where he was little known, he let himself be sold for three talents to Omphale, Queen of Lydia. She soon found out what a strong slave she had, who rid her land of robbers and beasts of prey as easily as another would bear wood and water. But when she knew that this was no other than the world-renowned Hercules, she would have kept him for a spouse rather than a servant. Then, alas! in the softness and luxury of eastern life, the hero forgot his manhood, and let Omphale make sport with him. While she took his club and lion-skin as toys, he put on woman's clothes and gauds to sit at her feet spinning wool, or amusing her and her maids with stories of how he had strangled snakes in his cradle, and laid low giants, and quelled monsters, and gone down to face the king of death in his dark abode.

So three years passed away in shameful ease; then at once Hercules came to his right mind, like one awakening from a dream. He tore off the womanish garments in shame; he dropped the distaff from his knotty hands; and, turning his back on the idle court of Omphale, strode forth once more to seek deeds that might become a hero. But again a woman was fated to be this strong man's undoing.

In his later wanderings he came to Calydon, and saw Deianira, daughter of King Oineus, to whom he bore a message from her brother Meleager in Hades. From him Hercules had heard of her beauty; now he loved her well and carried her away as his wife, after a hot fight for her with a rival wooer, the river-god Achelous, who changed himself into a snake and a bull, but in any form could not withstand the son of Zeus.

As if that beaten river-god would still do him an ill turn, his road brought him to a stream in flood, where the Centaur Nessus stood offering to carry wayfarers across on his back. For himself Hercules scorned such a

Hercules Defeats Achelous, who changed first into a bull, and then into a snake, but in vain for he could not resist Hercules. From an illuminated edition of *Metamorphoses* by Ovid, late fifteenth century.

ferry; he flung over his club and lion-skin on the farther bank, that he might lightly swim the swollen water; but his wife he trusted to Nessus. Then that rude Centaur, inflamed by her beauty, would have borne her off; but Hercules heard her cry, and with one of his evenomed arrows brought Nessus to the ground. In his death throes, the vengeful monster whispered to Deianira a lying tale: he bid her dip a shirt in his blood, and claimed that if ever she lost her husband's love, that should prove a charm to bring it back.

Hercules ended his labours by taking amends from those who in past years had done him wrong, among them King Eurytus, whom he conquered and slew, and made his daughter Iole a captive. When Deianira heard how her husband's old love lay in his power, she was moved by jealousy to try the spell of the Centaur's blood, which in truth had been poisoned by the hero's own deadly arrow. She sent him a shirt dipped in this venom, begging him to wear it as made by her hands. Without suspicion he put it on, when he came to offer sacrifices of thanksgiving for his victory.

Then, as soon as the fire on the altar had warmed the envenomed blood, burning pains seized him and shot through every vein, till, for once in his life, he could not but roar for agony. Vainly he struggled to pull off the fatal garment; it stuck to his skin like pitch, and he was fain to tear away the tortured flesh, beneath which his veins hissed and boiled as if melted by inward flames. In his rage he caught the servant who had innocently brought this gift from his wife, and hurled him into the sea. Seeing that he must die, with his last strength he tore down tree trunks to make a funeral pyre, on which he stretched himself, begging his companions to kindle it beneath his still living body. His armour-bearer, Philoctetes, alone had heart to do him this sad service, which Hercules rewarded with the gift of his deadly bow and arrows, that should one day be turned against Troy.

"Hera, thou art avenged: give me a stepmother's gift of death!" were his last words, as the flames rose crackling about him; and a terrible storm of thunder and lightning broke out above, through which Pallas-Athene's chariot bore the demigod to Olympus.

On the pyre lay the ashes of what part of him came from his mother. The immortal part he had from Zeus now dwelt in heaven. There even Hera's hatred died away, so that she welcomed him among the gods, and gave him in marriage her daughter Hebe, the spirit of eternal youth.

When poor Deianira knew what she had unwittingly done to her too dearly loved husband, she killed herself for remorse, goaded by the upbraiding of her own son Hyllus. By the dying wish of Hercules this son married Iole; and from them sprang a famous race of heroes, known to after-ages as the Heraclids.

But the children of Hercules long inherited their father's hard fortunes. They were chased from city to city by the hatred of Eurystheus, so

Hercules and Nessus at the River Evenus. Wall painting, first century A.D., from Pompeii. Nessus, the centaur who carried travellers across the river, tried to outrage Hercules' wife, Deianira, but Hercules heard her screaming and shot an arrow into the heart of the beast.

The Death of Hercules on Mount Oeta.
Terrible thunder and lightning broke
out as Hercules spoke his last words:
"Hera, thou art avenged: give me a
stepmother's gift of death!"

that they must wander over Greece under the guardianship of Iolaus, now grown old and feeble, yet ever faithful to the memory of his dead comrade and kinsman. At last Demophoon, son of Theseus, gave them refuge in Athens, and with Hyllus gathered an army to defend them against Eurystheus. An oracle declaring that a maiden of noble birth must be sacrificed as the price of victory, Macaria, daughter of Hercules and Deianira, did not fear to devote herself to death. And in the hot battle Iolaus prayed Zeus to give him back for one day the strength of his youth; then, his prayer being heard, no foe could stand before a champion worthy to follow that peerless hero. The host of Eurystheus was set to flight, and its lord brought to a miserable end.

Still the Heraclids found themselves dogged by evil fate, as if the sins of their great father rose up against them. It was long before the curse of the race seemed to have worn out. Not till generations had passed, were warriors of the blood of Hercules able to conquer the Peloponnesus and divide its kingdoms among their chiefs.

PYGMALION AND GALATEA

Pygmalion, king of Cyprus, had more fame as a sculptor than as a warrior. So devoted was he to his art that he cared not to marry, declaring that no living woman could be so beautiful as the figures he fashioned with his own hands. And at one ivory statue he wrought so long and so lovingly that it became the mistress of his heart, till he would have spent all he had in the world to give it breath as well as silent grace and beauty. All day he laboured to put new touches of perfection to the senseless form; and all night he lay sighing for the power to make it flesh and blood.

Galatea was the name he gave his statue, in vain hoping to call it to life. In vain he sought to kiss warmth and motion into its shapely limbs. He decked it with costly tissues, made its neck and arms sparkle with precious jewels, wreathed its cold head with flowers of every hue; but all in vain. The image remained an image, that seemed less fair the more he

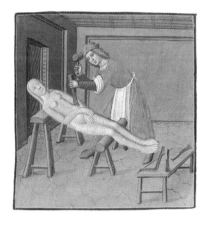

Pygmalion Fashioning Galatea, the sculpture with which he fell in love. From an illuminated edition of *Metamorphoses* by Ovid, late fifteenth century.

Pygmalion and the Image (left), by E. Burne-Jones, oil on canvas, 99 × 76.5 cm. (City Museum and Art Gallery, Birmingham, England.) "Aphrodite hath worked her miracle!"

Pygmalion, by Honoré Daumier. Caricature from the "Histoires Anciennes" series, in *Le Charivari*. "No living woman could be so beautiful as the figures I fashion."

hid its white form in gold and purple. There came the feast of Aphrodite, great goddess of the island. Then Pygmalion presented himself in her temple, bearing rich offerings and sending up a passionate prayer with the incense smoke that rose from the altar.

"Queen of love, take pity on one who has too long despised thy power! Give me for bride the work of my own hands; or, if that may not be, a maiden of earth as lovely as my Galatea!"

As if in favourable answer, three times the altar flame leaped up in the air, making Pygmalion's heart beat high with joyful hope. He hastened home to stand before the statue that a hundred times had almost cheated his eyes into belief it might be alive.

"Galatea!" he cried for the thousandth time, stretching out his arms; then had almost shrunk back in dread of what he so long desired.

For now as Pygmalion gazed, a change came over the ivory shape. Its breast heaved; its veins ran with blood; its eyes no longer stared upon him like stones. It was no cheat. He pressed the hand that grew warm and soft in his. He could feel the pulses throbbing under his touch. He smiled to the face that smiled back again. He spoke, and his Galatea's lips had breath to answer—

"Aphrodite hath worked her miracle!"

> "Speechless he stood, but she now drew anear,
> Simple and sweet as she was wont to be,
> And once again her silver voice rang clear,
> Filling his soul with great felicity;
> And thus she spoke, 'Wilt thou not come to me,
> O dear companion of my new-found life,
> For I am called thy lover and thy wife'."
>
> —W. Morris.

THE RAPE OF PERSEPHONE

The Rape of Persephone. While the unsuspecting maiden was gathering flowers, the earth opened, and she was carried off by Hades, King of the Underworld. From an illuminated edition of *Metamorphoses* by Ovid, late fifteenth century.

An ill trick it was Aphrodite played on gods and men when she bid her mischievous son shoot his dart at Pluto, that even in his gloomy kingdom should be known the power of love. From such a mountain-mouth as breathes fire and smoke over Sicily came forth the stern King of Hades, to drive in his iron chariot across that fair isle, where the ground heaves beneath fruitful crops, and ruin is strangely mingled with the richest green. There, in the Vale of Enna, his lowering looks fell upon Persephone, sweet daughter of Demeter, blooming like the flowers she plucked among her sportive companions. But she dropped her lapful of violets and lilies when that fearsome wooer caught her up into his chariot, striking his forked spear upon the ground, that opened in a dark cleft through which he bore her away to his dwelling in the nether world. A cry for help, too late, brought up Demeter to see that her beloved daughter had vanished from the face of the earth.

"Persephone! Persephone!" she cried in vain. No answer came but the rumble of the earthquake and the stifled roar of the volcano hailing that tyrant's retreat to his kingdom underground.

All day the woeful mother sought her lost child, and all night she went calling Persephone's name, lit by torches kindled at the fires of Etna. Many a day, indeed, she now wandered over land and sea, but neither sun nor moon could show her the darling face, never forgotten in her heart. At last, coming back to Sicily, she found a trace of Persephone, what but her girdle floating on a stream into which one of the girl's playmates had wept herself away, and could give only such silent token of her friend's fate!

But the nymph of another stream had power to speak, fair Arethusa, who, pursued by the river-god Alpheus under the sea, had fled to Ortygia, and there was changed by Artemis into a sacred fountain. She in pity told Demeter how, when drawing her springs from the deep caverns under-

Persephone's Girdle Floating in the Stream. Persephone's mother, demented by her daughter's disappearance, searched the earth in vain. From an illuminated edition of *Metamorphoses* by Ovid, late fifteenth century.

The Return of Persephone (right), by Frederick Leighton. Oil on canvas, 201 × 150 cm, 1891. (Leeds City Art Gallery, England.) "On her return, the very land grew and blossomed again with joy."

Proserpine (previous page), by Dante Gabriel Rosetti. Oil on canvas, 125 × 61 cm, 1874. (The Tate Gallery, London.) Proserpine (Persephone) bites into the seeds of a pomegranate, symbolising her bondage to the King of the Underworld.

ground, she had seen young Persephone throned by Pluto's side as the queen of Hades, adorned with gems and gold in place of flowers, and had through that chill darkness heard her sighing for the sunlit vale whence death's king so roughly snatched her away. What power could bring her back from his cold embrace?

In wild despair Demeter cursed the earth, and chiefly the soil of Sicily that had swallowed up her child. Her tears fell as a plague upon field and grove, so that they no more yielded fruit for man or beast. The people wasted away in famine, crying upon the gods, who feared to lose the reverence and sacrifices due to them. Zeus himself pled with Demeter in vain: she would not return to her seat on Olympus, but went madly up and down the world, scathing and blighting where she was wont to bless.

"If a mother's tears touch thee not, be mindful of a father's pride!" was ever her prayer to Zeus. "She is thy daughter as well as mine, doomed to so untimely fate; and thy honour as well as my woe calls for redress against the insolent robber of our child."

At last the father of the gods was fain to appease this ceaseless suppliant. He sent Hermes to fetch Persephone from the nether world and restore her to her mother's arms; yet so it might be only if she had eaten nothing in the kingdom of Pluto. Alas! that very day she had been tempted to taste the seeds of a pomegranate; and thus was she still held in the power of her grudging spouse.

Once more the miserable mother filled heaven with her entreaties, and earth with her wrath. Again Zeus gave a decree that should content both his brother and the goddess of fruitfulness. Persephone's life must henceforth be divided between her mother and her husband, and with each of them she should spend half the year: no otherwise might it be than life and death for her in turns.

Joyful was Demeter to clasp her fair daughter, brought back from the gloomy realm of Pluto; and glad was the earth of her joy. For now again the land grew green like a jewel set in its rim of blue sea; the withered trees budded and blossomed; the naked mountains were clothed with leaves; sweet flowers sprang up in valleys for children to gather freshly; the fields and gardens bore goodly food for man, and all the world smiled back to the bright sky of summer.

But, in turn, came year by year their darkening days, when the goddess gave up her daughter to that tyrant of the shades. Then all the earth must mourn with Demeter, laying aside the gay garlands of summer and the rich robes of autumn for wan weeds that ill kept out the winter cold, till again the welcome heralds of spring let men hail Persephone returning to her mother's arms. And so it goes with the world, while men still live and die.

Other wondrous tales men tell of what befell Demeter in those weary wanderings, to and fro, when long she sought her vanished child over the face of the earth. As this: that coming one day to a cottage, disguised as an old beggar woman, she was scornfully given a bowl of mush at the door,

Persephone was known in ancient Greece as *Kore* (the Daughter). A marble statue, from the first half of the sixth century B.C.

The Goddess Demeter Gives Triptolemus an Ear of Corn, a promise of plenty and abundance. Attributed to Phidias, *c.* 440 B.C. Votive relief, found at Eleusis, Greece. (National Museum, Athens.)

where the son of the house, like the rude boy he was, laughed to see how hungrily she ate such humble food; then the seeming crone flung the bowl in his face with an angry word, at which, lo! he had been changed into a spotted lizard, to teach him and his that poverty may hide a goddess.

But another home gave less churlish welcome to this beggar, old and poor. At Eleusis, in Greece, it was that a kindly housewife took her in, and would have had her stay as nurse to the new-born son, named *Triptolemus*. Bereaved Demeter came to love this child almost as her own, so that she was minded to bestow on him in secret the gift of immortality. His own mother, waking up one night, stood amazed to find that nurse holding her babe in the flames of the fire; then with screams of terror she snatched him away, knowing not how his limbs had been bathed in nectar, and a charm breathed over him so that the fire should but temper his life to deathlessness. Now the stranger shone forth by the hearth as a goddess, to tell what purpose it was had thus been brought to nought; and forthwith she passed away upon her long quest.

But when her mind was set at ease by the return of Persephone, Demeter sought out that nursling at Eleusis to show through him new favour to mortals. In her dragon-chariot she sent Triptolemus out with the gift of corn for men, and to teach them the use of the plough and the sickle, so that no more should they be in danger of famine. And in his native land she set on foot the sacred *Eleusinian* festival, by which for ages to come its people should remember Demeter and Persephone.

ORPHEUS AND EURYDICE

Orpheus and Eurydice, by Frederick Leighton, oil on canvas, 1864. (Leighton House Museum, London.) These two fated lovers were destined to enjoy only the briefest moments of happiness together.

Orpheus the Thracian was famed as sweetest minstrel of old. Son of the muse Calliope, he was born under Mount Rhodope, yet often wandered about Olympus, home of the gods, enchanting also with his song the wooded slopes on *Parnassus* and the sacred spring of Helicon. The tale goes how when, with the skill taught by his mother-muse, he struck the golden lyre given him by Apollo, fierce beasts of the forest would come forth charmed to tameness; the rushing streams stood still to listen; and the very rocks and trees were drawn after that witching music, that softened the hearts of savage men.

The singer who could breathe life into a stone, readily won the heart of fair Eurydice, not the less since he had shown himself brave as well as gifted when he followed Jason on the quest of the Golden Fleece. But all too short was the happiness of that loving pair. As she danced at their bridal feast, a venomous snake, gliding through the grass, stung the heel of Eurydice, so that she died on the night she was wedded.

The lamenting husband bore her to the grave, playing mournful airs that moved the hearts of all who followed that funeral train. Then, life seeming to him dark as death without his Eurydice, Orpheus pressed on to the very gates of Hades, seeking her where no living man might enter

Parnassus (left), by Andrea Mantegna, oil on canvas, 160 × 192 cm, *c.* 1497. (The Louvre, Paris.) "When Orpheus played his golden lyre, the very rocks, trees and streams stood still to listen."

Eurydice Bitten by a Snake (below), school of Giorgone (Accademia Carrara, Bergamo, Italy). A venomous snake stung Eurydice on her wedding-day and she died that same night. Her grief-stricken husband, Orpheus, followed her into the underworld.

till the day of his own doom. But at this man's tuneful strains, Charon silently ferried him across the Styx, that black stream that divides our sunlit world from the cold realms of Pluto. So moving were the notes of his lyre that the iron bars slid back of themselves, and *Cerberus*, the three-headed guard of death's gloomy portal, sank down without showing his teeth, to let the lulling music pass. Without check or challenge Orpheus stole boldly into the world of the shades, flitting about him from all sides to fix their dim eyes on the man who could work such a spell even among the dead.

Fearsome and gruesome were the sights he saw in the dark caves of Tartarus, yet through them he held on undismayed, straining his eyes after Eurydice alone. He came past the daughters of Danaus, who, all save one, had stabbed their husbands on the wedding night, and for such a crime must do eternal penance by vainly pouring water into a sieve; but, as the Thracian singer went by, they had a brief respite from their bootless task, turning on him looks which he gave not back. So, too, his music made a moment's peace for Tantalus, that once rich and mighty king, that for unspeakable offence against the gods was doomed to suffer burning thirst in a lake whose waters ever fled from his lips, and in his hungry eyes bloomed clusters of ripe fruit shrinking and withering as he stretched out his hand to clutch them; and over his head hung a huge stone threatening in vain to crush him out of his misery. Again, Orpheus passed where Sisyphus, for his life's burden of wickedness, had to roll uphill a heavy rock always slipping from his arms to spin down to the bottom: he, too, could pause to wipe his hot brow as the singer's voice fell on his ears like balm. Nor did the spell of music fail to stop Ixion's wheel, bound to which that treacherous murderer must for ever whirl through the fiery air in

Cerberus, by William Blake. Watercolour drawing on paper, 37 × 53 cm, 1824–1827. (The Tate Gallery, London.) Cerberus, the three-headed hound of Hades, guarded the entrance to the underworld.

unpitied torment. Then for once, they say, were tears drawn to the dry eyes of the Furies, those three chastising sisters, whose very name men fear to speak.

But Orpheus looked not aside, and the thin ghosts ever made way for him as he pressed on till he came before the throne where the dark-browed King of Hades sat beside his queen Persephone, her fair face veiled by the shadows of that dire abode. Then, striking his softest notes, the suppliant minstrel raised a chant to stir the hardest heart, beseeching its sovereign for once to loose the bonds of death.

"Love", he sang, "gives me strength to seek the shades before my time; love, that if tales be true, has had power even here, when stern Pluto came forth to win a bride snatched from the world of life. Let me take back my loved one, doomed too soon by fate! Or, if that may not be, oh! dread king, in mercy accept two victims for one, nor bid me return alone to the upper air."

Black-browed Pluto nodded to his prayer, when Persephone whispered a pitiful word in her consort's ear. Then the lyre of Orpheus was silenced by a hollow voice proclaiming through the vaulted halls a boon for once granted to mortal man. All Hades held its breath to hear.

"So be it! Back to the world above, and Eurydice shall follow thee as they shadow! But halt not, speak not, turn not to look behind, till ye have gained the upper air, or never mayst thou see her face again. Begone without delay, and on thy silent path thou wilt not be alone."

In grateful awe, the husband of Eurydice turned his back upon death's throne, taking his way through the chill gloom towards a faint glimmer that marked the gate of Hades. Fain would he have looked round to make sure that Eurydice came behind him, fain would he have halted to listen for her footfall. But now all was still as death, save his own hasty steps echoing dreadfully as he pressed on to the light that shone clearer and clearer before him like a star of hope. Then doubt and impatience clouded his mind, so that he could not trust the word of a god. He had not yet gained the gate, when, giving way to eager desire, he turned his head

Orpheus and Eurydice at the Gates of Hell. "Giving way to desire, he turned and saw her shrouded form . . ." From an illuminated edition of *Metamorphoses* by Ovid, late fifteenth century.

Orpheus Stoned by the Maenads (left). Engraving from an illustrated edition of *Metamorphoses* by Ovid. Published in 1683 in Amsterdam. The Maenads were frenzied female disciples of Dionysus. They stoned Orpheus to the ground and broke his lyre in pieces.

Bacchus, also known as Dionysus, was the god of wine. Lead statue, eighteenth century, by Van Nost. Photographed by Edwin Smith in the 1960s. (The Theatre, Rousham, Oxford, England.)

Orpheus, by Odilon Redon, after 1913 pastel, 69 × 56 cm. (The Cleveland Museum of Art.) Orpheus' tomb became a sacred shrine on which the nightingales sang more sweetly than elsewhere.

and saw indeed behind him the shrouded form of her he loved so fondly.

"Eurydice!" he cried, stretching out his arms, but they clasped the cold thin air; and only a sigh came back to him, as her dim shape melted away into the darkness.

In vain the twice-bereaved lover made Hades ring with Eurydice's name. He was never to see her more while he lived. Out of his senses for despair, he found himself thrust into the daylight, alone. There he lay like an image, for days unable to speak, or to sing, with no desire but to starve himself back to death.

At last he rose and took his way into the world of men. Now he went silent, the strings of his lyre broken like his heart. He shunned all dwellings and scenes of joy, nor would he look upon the face of women, though many a maid smiled kindly to bid him forget his lost Eurydice. Henceforth, his solitary haunts were the mountain forests of Thrace, where beasts rather than men would be his companions among the rough thickets and trees.

But ere long, as he would have retuned his lyre to strains of woe, the rocks rang with a clamorous din, and forth upon him burst a troop of

Mænads, women frenzied by the rites of Dionysus, to whom, with jangling cymbals and clanging horns, they yelled a shrill chorus *Evoe, Evoe!* Clothed in fawnskins, and garlanded with vine leaves, they danced towards the stranger; but Orpheus rose in horror to fly from their flushed faces, nor heeded the wild outcry with which they called on him to join their revel. Furious at this affront, the maddened votaries of Bacchus followed him like fierce hunters closing on a deer. They stoned Orpheus to the ground, they broke his lyre in pieces, and, their drunken rage heated by the sight of blood, that ruthless crew ended by tearing their disdainer in pieces. His limbs were flung into a stream which bore them to the sea; and they tell how his head, still breathing Eurydice's name, was washed ashore on the isle of Lesbos, there to be buried by the Muses in a tomb that became a sacred shrine, on which the nightingales sang more sweetly than elsewhere.

MIDAS

Midas, king of Phrygia, was rich above all men in the world, yet, like others who have much, his heart was set on more. Once he had the chance to do a service to a god, when in his garden was found old Silenus, who, strayed from the train of his patron Dionysus, had lain down here to sleep off a drunken bout. Midas sportively bound the wandering reveller with roses, and, after filling him with the meat and drink he loved, took him back to the god of wine; then so well pleased was Dionysus to see that jovial companion, that he bid the friendly king choose any reward he liked to ask. Midas did not think twice.

"Grant me this boon then," he cried eagerly: "that whatever I touch may turn to gold!"

"So be it!" laughed the god, pledging him in a cup of wine; and Midas left his presence exulting to know that henceforth he would enjoy boundless wealth.

Impatient to test his new-given power, as he walked through the woods he tore off a twig, and lo! at his touch it turned to yellow gold. He picked up stones from the path, then they, too, became pure gold, and every clod he handled was at once a glittering nugget; he grasped an ear of corn to find it hard as gold; and when he plucked fruit or flowers they were like the apples of the Hesperides, so that soon his attendants went groaning under the burden of gold he gathered on the way. Weighed down by his golden robes, he himself would fain have been borne along, but when he mounted a mule it stood a lifeless image, and the litter on which they laid him was too heavy for the strength of all his men. Almost beside himself with pride and greed, he got home to his palace, where, as he brushed through the portal, its posts turned to golden pillars; and when he threw himself on the nearest seat, it was henceforth such a costly throne as any king in the world might envy.

Hercules and Silenus depicted on an amphora, Rhyton from Panagyurishte (Thracian treasure), fourth to third century B.C. (Archaelogical Museum, Plovdiv, Bulgaria.) The satyr, Silenus, was a part-bestial, part-human disciple of Dionysus. He was often described as a jovial old man with a bald head, a puck nose, and a wine-bag as fat as himself.

Fatigued by his journey and its excitements, Midas called for food. Obedient menials made haste to spread a table, while others brought basins in which as their lord plunged his hands, the water froze forthwith into golden ice. So it was when he sat down to eat. He smiled to see how his plates and bowls changed to gold, as beseemed; but his smile became a frown when the first savoury mouthful met his lips as tasteless metal. In vain he tried to swallow such rich fare; the sweetest morsel crunched between his teeth like ashes; and when he would have drained a cup of wine, the drink was solid gold.

Tormented by hunger and thirst, he rose from that mockery of a banquet, for once envying the poorest kitchen-boy in his palace. It was no comfort to visit the growing mass of his treasures; the very sight of gold began to sicken him. If he embraced his children, if he struck a slave, their bodies turned in an instant to golden statues. All around glared hateful yellow in his eyes. It was a relief when darkness came to hide that now-abhorred wealth. Then, flinging off his heavy golden robes, he sank with a sigh upon a soft couch that at once grew hard and cold; and there he tossed restless all night, the richest and the most wretched man alive.

In sleepless despair, with the first light of dawn King Midas hastened to Dionysus, earnestly beseeching him to take back his gift of splendid misery.

"So men's dearest wishes oft prove unwise!" railed the god. "But once more I grant thee thy desire. Seek out the source of the Pactolus, and by bathing in its pure waters thou mayst undo the spell laid upon thee."

Scarcely waiting to thank him, Midas set off for that healing stream. Driven on by the gnawings of hunger, over mountain and plain he panted till he came to the Pactolus, whose sandy bed was streaked with gold

Apollo and Marsyas, by Pietro Vanucci, called il Perugino, 1448–1523. Wood, 39 × 29 cm. (The Louvre, Paris.) The satyr, Marsyas, was a gifted musician but his talent was envied by the jealous god, Apollo, who put Marsyas to a terrible death.

The Feast of Midas (right), by Lucas van Valkenborch, 1530–1597, oil. (Pushkin Museum, Moscow.) Midas' joy quickly turned to grief when he realised he could neither eat nor drink, for all that he touched turned to gold.

The Triumph of Bacchus, by Cornelis de Vos, 1585–1651. Canvas, 180 × 295 cm. (Prado, Madrid.) "Crowned with vine leaves and grapes, carrying a wand wreathed with ivy or vines . . ."

wherever he trod; and men say that scales of gold may still be turned up to mark his footsteps. When he reached its cool fountain and hurled into it his fevered body, the crystal water was stained as if by gold. But no sooner had his head plunged beneath it, than that fatal gift was washed away; and to his unspeakable joy Midas came out able to eat and drink once again, like other men.

This king was not always so fortunate in his dealings with the gods. Cured of his greed for gold, yet no wiser in his mind, he took to roaming the green woods, and there came upon Pan at strife with the great Apollo. For that rude Satyr had presumed to boast his pipe of reeds against the god's lute; and they took Midas for judge which of them made the sweetest music. After listening to their strains, the dull-eared mortal gave judgment for Pan; then Apollo, in displeasure, punished him by decking his head with the ears of an ass, even as the Muses spitefully turned the daughters of Pierus into birds, when these mortal maidens would have contended with them in song on Mount Helicon.

The first pool into which Midas looked showed him how shamefully he had been transformed; but this time he could hope no favour from an angry god. Slinking into his palace by night, the king would have hid from all that he bore those long, hairy ears. His head he kept wrapped night and day in a turban such as makes a shield against the sun for men of the hot East. None knew why Midas went thus arrayed, save only his barber, to whom he could not but disclose the truth, binding him by oaths and threats never to breathe it to human ear. But the barber, for his part, could not bear the weight of such a secret which he must not tell. Itching to let it out, yet fearing his master's wrath, he stole down to the lonely bank of the river and scooped out a hole, into which he whispered *"Midas has ass's ears"*, hoping to be heard by no man. But where he had opened the ground, there grew up a clump of reeds that, as often as they were stirred by the wind, kept on murmuring, *"Midas has ass's ears"*.

THE ARGONAUTS
Jason's Youth

In a cave high up the rocky and snowy sides of Mount Pelion dwelt Cheiron, oldest and wisest of the Centaurs, that wondrous race that were half-horse and half-man. When the brute strength of his lower part began to fail, the white-bearded Centaur's head was richly stored with knowledge and experience, and his hands had rare skill in playing on a golden harp, to the music of which he gave forth wise counsels in human speech. So great was his fame that many a king's and hero's son came to be trusted to his care for rearing in all that beseemed a noble youth. From him they had lessons in duty, to fear the gods, to reverence old age, and to stand by one another in pain and hardship. So in all the world there were no goodlier lads than they who grew up under the care of Cheiron to be both skilful and strong, modest as well as brave, and fitted to rule by having rightly known to obey.

Among that youthful fellowship, goodliest in his day was Jason, a boy of princely race, nay, a king's son by right. For his father Æson had been born heir of Iolcos, yet let this kingdom be stolen from him by his wicked half-brother Pelias, who would have slain Jason to make that wrongdoing sure. But Æson had saved the child by flight, hiding him in Cheiron's cave where for years Jason little guessed his true heritage.

When the sturdy lad had shot to full stature, and his mind turned eagerly to the wide world in which he might prove his manhood, old Cheiron saw the time come to let him know the secret of his birth, and how he was destined to avenge on Pelias the wrong done to his father. The young hero heard in amazement; then not a day would he delay in setting out on the adventure in store for him. Taking leave of his envious playmates, he dutifully received his old master's parting counsel.

"I need not wish thee fearless before enemies; but remember how it becomes a king's son to be friendly to all other men, and helpful in their hour of need."

The youth's heart beat high with hope, as under the bright morning sun he took his way down the mountain, where every step brought him nearer in view of the unknown world below. On the bank of a rushing

Cheiron, the oldest and wisest of the centaurs, attracted many young disciples who flocked to hear his teaching. From *The Heroes* by Charles Kingsley, 1868, London.

river he found an old woman in mean rags, who rocked herself feebly as she sat and cried out beseechingly—

"Alas! who will carry me across?"

"My shoulders are broad enough for such a light load!" said he heartily. "Up with thee, old mother, and, the gods aiding, I will bear thee safe!" Without more ado, before he could raise a hand to lift her up, the seeming helpless beggar sprang on his back; and with her arms clinging round his neck, he strode boldly into the stream. As he scrambled to shore, all dripping and breathless, she sprang from his back to take on a wondrously altered guise. There stood before him a tall and stately form, like no daughter of woman, her rags changed to jewelled robes, and her eyes now smiling on him so radiantly that he knew her as of divine race.

"Yes," she said, reading his mind. "I am indeed Hera, the queen of heaven, to whom thou hast done such service unaware. In thine own hour of need, call upon me, and see if a goddess can be grateful."

Speechless, the youth fell upon his knees, his eyes dazzled by the vision of glory that, as he gazed, went up in a shining cloud; and when he could see clearly, he was alone on the river bank.

Jason took his way onwards to a city whose towers stood out before him upon the plain. But now he limped along more slowly, for he found he had lost one of his sandals, left sticking in the slimy bed of the torrent, where a sharp stone had cut his bare foot. He bound up his hurt with soft leaves, and held on through shade and sunshine till towards evening he reached the gate of Iolcos.

There he found all astir with a great feast held by Pelias in honour of the gods. Many an eye was cast curiously on this comely youth, as he wandered through the streets, sun-tanned and dusty from the long way. He thought these trim citizens despised him for being but half-shod, for he knew not what was known to them, how an oracle had foretold that Pelias should lose his ill-gotten kingdom to a stranger who came wearing but one sandal.

Seeking his way to the palace, he presented himself before Pelias, who, amid all his royal state, might well start at the sight of this half-barefooted youth, since night and day his guilty mind never forgot what sign was to mark the avenger.

"I am Jason, son of Æson, come to claim my rightful heritage," declared the youth boldly.

The king's heart sank within him but, hiding his dismay, he made a show of welcoming this nephew, and bid him sit down at the feast beside his own fair daughters.

Simple and honest himself, Jason was won by his uncle's fine words and by the charms of his new-found cousins. Their seeming kindness turned his head, so that he let his heart go out to them. He ate and drank among them friendly, then, flushed with wine, listened eagerly to the minstrels who cheered the banquet. A song that set his pulses beating was the tale of the Golden Fleece: how Phrixus and Helle, a king's son and

Temple of Hera at Paestum, Italy. Mid-fifth century B.C. Photographed by Edwin Smith in the 1960s. During the fifth century B.C., Paestum or Posidonia was a powerful and flourishing city. The ruins of two Doric temples at Paestum are some of the most remarkable remains of antiquity.

Hera Appearing to Jason. "The withered crone suddenly transformed into the stately, radiant shape of Hera herself." From *The Heroes* by Charles Kingsley, 1868, London.

The Golden Ram Took Them on his Back and Vanished. Phrixus and Helle, brother and sister, were to be sacrificed to Zeus, but escaped on a golden ram who rode away through the air. Only Phrixus landed safely: Helle fell into the sea, afterwards named the Hellespont. Illustration by George Soper for *The Heroes* by Charles Kingsley, 1910, London.

daughter, were persecuted by their cruel stepmother Ino; how they fled from her on a golden ram, sent by a friendly god; how poor Helle, turning giddy as they flew over land and sea, fell from its back into the Hellespont, that has ever afterwards been known by her name; but Phrixus safely reached Colchis at the farther end of the dark Euxine Sea; how he sacrificed the ram to Zeus, and hung up its fleece in a sacred grove by the river of the Colchians, among whom henceforth he lived and died. There it was jealously treasured by Æetes, king of that distant land, whose own life, said an oracle, depended on its safe keeping, so that he had it guarded night and day by a sleepless serpent, as by other perils no hero had been found bold enough to face; but never would the ghost of dead Phrixus be laid till the Golden Fleece were won back to his kinsmen in Greece. This song had been sung by command of Pelias; and keenly he watched his nephew's flashing eyes as the moving tale was told. "Ah!" exclaimed the crafty king, "time was when I would have dared all for such a prize. But I am old, and the sons of our day are not as their fathers. Where lives the man who will venture to bring back the Golden Fleece?"

"Here!" cried Jason, leaping to his feet. "I will seek the Fleece, if I have to pay for it with my life."

His cunning uncle made haste to embrace him, with feigned pride and joy in a youth worthy of their heroic stock. Yes, let him bring the Golden Fleece to Iolcos; and he himself would gladly give up the kingdom to the hero of such a deed! So he promised, secretly trusting that his brave kinsman would never come back from that perilous errand; and thus by guile and flattery he hoped to make himself sure of his stolen power.

Jason sought the aid of a cunning shipwright called Argus, who from the tall pines of Mount Pelion built him a fifty-oared ship, so strong that it could bear the buffeting of winds and waves, yet so light that it might be carried on the shoulders of its crew. This was named the *Argo*, after its builder, a craftsman inspired by Athene.

For comrades Jason gathered the best and bravest of the Grecian youth, sons of gods and men, a band henceforth to be known as the

Pelias Sending Forth Jason. "Where lives he who will bring back the Golden Fleece?" Illustrations by Flaxman and others. From *Stories from the Greek Tragedians* by A.J. Church, 1880, London.

Argonauts. Among them were Hercules, the twin-brethren Castor and Pollux, Theseus, Orpheus, Peleus, Admetus, and many more, fifty in all, one to each oar of the galley. Argus himself made one of the crew, Tiphys was their steersman and sharp-eyed Lynceus their pilot. They launched forth the *Argo* into the blue sea, its prow set towards that far-off eastern land whence they must tear the Golden Fleece.

The Voyage to Colchis

'Twere long to tell all that hindered those heroes on their far course, and how one and another were cut off by mishaps, never to reach the Colchian land. Turning from the shores of Thessaly, they stood across the Ægean Sea to the rocky island of Lemnos.

[Here they are ensnared by the women of the island, who through jealousy have slaughtered their menfolk and, repentant, welcome the sailors with open arms. Jason and his crew give way to their charms. It takes Hercules to tear them away.]

Bending afresh to their oars, they passed through the Hellespont and came to a haven in the Propontis Sea, where Cyzicus, the young king of the Doliones, received them gladly and would have them stay to his wedding feast. But Hercules, again on watch in the ship, saw how here too there was a snare set. For a race of giant savages came down from the hills, and were blocking up the harbour mouth with huge stones, when Hercules gave the alarm, and with his arrows kept off these foemen, who fell or fled when the whole band had gathered to defend their ship.

Soon they were to lose stout Hercules, who more than once had served them so well. As he tugged at his oar in the stormy waves, it broke, and not easily could another be found to match his brawny arms. When next they went on shore and his companions were being feasted by the hospitable Mysians, Hercules strode off into the forest to cut for himself a new oar from some tall pine tree. With him went the beautiful boy Hylas, whom he loved like a son, and also another of the crew named Polyphemus. While Hercules stripped himself to fell the tree he had chosen, young Hylas turned aside to a spring from which he would have drawn water for their supper. In this spring dwelt a bevy of water nymphs, who, as they saw the boy leaning over with his brazen pitcher, were so taken by his beauty, that they cast their arms round him and dragged him down into the water, never again to be seen of men. Polyphemus heard his last cry, and hastened to tell Hercules that the lad was being caught by robbers or wild beasts.

In vain these two searched for him through the forest, shouting and raging against the unseen foe who had laid hands on the hero's darling. Meanwhile their shipmates impatiently awaited them, for the wind had turned fair. When the hours passed and Hercules came not, they fell to quarrelling among themselves, for some said they should not go without that tower of strength, but others were for leaving him behind. So, in the

The Good Ship Argo ". . . leapt up from the sand upon the rollers and plunged onward like a gallant horse." Illustration by George Soper for *The Heroes* by Charles Kingsley, 1910, London.

end, they did, and with quiet minds after the sea-god Glaucus had risen from the waves to disclose to them how Hercules was not destined to share the gaining of the Golden Fleece. That hero had glory enough awaiting him elsewhere. [On their next landing, the Argonauts are challenged to a bout of boxing with the king of the Bebrycians. Later, on arrival at the home of the blind king Phineus, they chase away the Harpies that have been snatching his food.] In gratitude, he warned them of dangers that await the Argonauts on their course. The first are the Symplegades, two islands of floating ice-rock that would open like a monster's jaws to close upon their ship and crush it, unless they could speed through at the nick of time. By his advice they took a dove on board to show them the opening of the perilous passage. Loosing the dove, they saw it fly through those heaving rocks, that closed to snap off but its last feather and again drew asunder in haste; then the Argonauts pulled hard at their oars, and their wary steersman brought them darting between the icy walls that in another moment would have clashed upon them.

Holding their way along the coast of the black Pontus, they met with other mischances and delays. Where king Lycus entertained them at the mouth of the Acheron, Idmon, the diviner, blind to his own fate, was slain by the tusk of a wild boar. Here, too, their steersman Tiphys died of short sickness; and days were spent on the funeral piles. Well for the heroes, it may be, that they did not linger in the land of the Amazons, for these fierce women were more ready to wield sword and spear than distaff or needle. Also they skirted the coast of the Chalybes, those sooty iron smiths that night and day forge arms in the service of Ares. Next, standing out to sea, they were attacked by a flock of prodigious birds, called the Stymphalides, that cast their brazen feathers from them like darts to wound the men at their oars. But while half of them rowed on, the other half stood on guard, and raised such a din by smiting spear upon shield, that the birds were scared away, and the *Argo* could anchor safely by an island near the east end of this sea.

Here they drew near to their goal, and now they fell in with new comrades that would stead them well. [These are the four sons of Phrixus, shipwrecked on this isle when their father brought the Golden Fleece to Colchis. They agree to guide the Argonauts to the home of Aetes, the cruel king who guards the Fleece.] So at last the *Argo* entered the Phasis, river of Colchis, and by its bank her crew saw the dark grove sacred to Ares, in which gleamed that Golden Fleece they had come to fetch away.

The Winning of the Fleece

Leaving most of his men to guard their ship, Jason went forward to the city with a few companions, among them the four sons of Phrixus, who were here at home. Forth to meet them came King Æetes, for from his towers he had seen the *Argo* reach the Colchian shore; and an evil dream had warned him of her errand. With him came his young son Absyrtus,

Blind Phineas and the Harpies, disgusting birds with the heads of maidens, long claws and faces pale with hunger. Phineas was delivered from them by the Argonauts. Greek Kalpis, *c.* 480 B.C. (J. Paul Getty Museum, California.)

Hylas and the Nymphs (following page), by J.W. Waterhouse. Oil on canvas, 98 × 163 cm, 1896. (Manchester City Art Gallery, England.) "They were so taken by his beauty that they dragged him into the water, never to be seen again."

also his two daughters, Medea the witch-maiden, and Chalciope, the widow of Phrixus. Right glad was she to see her sons, whom she had mourned as lost. Medea looked kindly upon Jason, for in a dream she had foreseen his coming, and no such goodly man could she see in Colchis. Their dark-minded sire had little joy to hail those strangers, yet hiding his ill will, he led them to the lordly halls of his dwelling, and set food and drink before them.

Not till the guests had eaten, did he ask what brought them to Colchis. Then with Medea's eyes ever fixed upon him, Jason told of their voyage, and all the perils they had come through for the sake of the Golden Fleece, which he boldly demanded as their reward. To this the frowning king made answer:–

"Verily, it is a vain errand to come on from so far. What ye have borne is but child's play to that which the man must dare who would prove himself worthy of such a prize. Listen, stranger, if thou have the heart even to hear the trial appointed for that rash hand that may not touch sacred things till he have proved himself more than man. Two brazen-hoofed bulls, breathing fire from their nostrils, must he tame and yoke to a plough. Thus must he plough four acres of stony field, and sow the furrows with the teeth of a venomous dragon. From these teeth will spring up forthwith a crop of armed foemen, to be mowed down before they can slay him. All this must he accomplish between the sun's rising and setting; then if he still dare, he may strive with the serpent that guards the Fleece night and day. Art thou the man?"

Jason's heart quailed within him as he listened to this tale of terrors, that indeed seemed more than mortal strength could affront. But he showed no fear, and, trusting in the favour of Hera and his own arm, he let the king know that he was ready for that ordeal, the sooner the better. Since it must take the whole day, this was put off till next morning; and the hero went back to his ship to rest before confronting those unearthly adversaries.

But while he slept, others in Colchis were wakeful. Chalciope wept in sore dismay, fearing lest, if Jason failed in his attempt, Æetes would slay all the Argonauts, and among them her sons who had guided their ship to Colchis. Therefore she sought the aid of her witch sister to work some spell on behalf of the strangers. Nor did Medea need persuading to pity, for at first sight she had loved Jason, and was minded to save him from the death designed by her cruel father. At nightfall she wandered among the woods gathering herbs and roots, out of whose juices she knew the art to make a magic salve, that for one whole day could keep a man scathless from fire and sword, and temper all his arms against the doughtiest stroke. Her charms duly worked, wrapped in a veil she went towards the harbour at the earliest peep of dawn, and there met Jason coming forth to see the sun rise once more, if never again.

"Wilt thou go to death?" whispered a veiled woman in his ear.

"I had not come to Colchis, did I fear death," answered Jason.

Combat Between Greeks and Amazons.
"These fierce women . . . more ready to wield sword and spear than distaff or needle." From *Manual of Mythology* by A.S. Murray, 1873, London.

"A bold heart alone will not avail. But one friend hast thou in this land, else thou wert lost," murmured the witch-maiden; and Jason knew her voice for that of the king's daughter whose dark eyes had met his so kindly. Hastily she gave him to understand how by her aid he might pass through the sore ordeal unhurt. Then the longer he listened, the more ready he was to trust her counsels, daughter of an enemy as she was. When in whispers she had told him all he must do, Medea put into his hands the magical salve, and fled back to her father's house as day began to break.

Jason lost no time in putting her spell to the proof. After bathing in the sea, he anointed himself from head to foot with that salve, also his

Jason Against the Brazen-footed Bulls.
Behind, Jason pitches a huge stone amidst the warriors. Engraving from an illustrated edition of *Metamorphoses*, by Ovid, published in 1683 in Amsterdam.

shield, his helmet, and all his weapons. This done, he let his comrades try their utmost upon him arrayed in the charmed armour. The strongest of them hacked at his spear without being able to break it with the sharpest sword; the mightiest blows made no dint on his polished shield; and he stood like a rock against the brawniest wrestler of the band. Seeing, then, how Medea had been true with him so far, he did not doubt to follow out her bidding to the end; so his heart was high as he presented himself to the king at sunrise.

"Hast thou not repented?" asked Æetes with a sneer. "I had hoped to find thee stolen away through the night with all thy presumptuous crew. It is no will of mine that a stranger must perish miserably. Bethink thee once again!" warned the King.

"The sun is in the sky; and I am ready," answered Jason.

Without more ado, the king led him to a field where were laid out the brazen yoke, the iron plough, and the goad with which he must tame those fiery bulls, whose bellowing could be heard from their stable underground. All the beholders drew back, while Jason stuck sword and spear in the earth, hung to them his helmet, and, throwing off his mantle, stood nude like a marble statue with only his shield in hand.

Out came the brazen-footed bulls so suddenly as seeming to rise from the ground, that shook beneath them as they bounded upon Jason, snorting red flames from their nostrils, and roaring like thunder amid a cloud of hot smoke. But the hero fled not nor flinched at their onset. He held up his shield, against which they dashed their iron horns in vain, and behind it he stood unhurt by their scorching breath. All other eyes were half-blinded in the smoke and dust, but they could see anon how the hero caught one bull by the horn to bring it on its back by sheer strength, and how he flung down the other to its knees, wrestling against both of them with hand and foot. They being thus overthrown, he forced upon their necks the strong yoke, and harnessed them to the heavy plough, and, goading them forward, though they bellowed and struggled like a storm wind, he ploughed up the field with deep and straight furrows, to the wonder of all looking on and the secret joy of Medea, who in the background kept muttering magic spells on his behalf.

Even scowling Æetes could not but marvel at such feats. But wrath was in his heart as he saw half the appointed task done, and still it was but noon. Yet he trusted that the other half were beyond this bulltaming champion's strength. When the weary beasts had been driven back to their underground cave, he gave Jason a helmet full of dragons' teeth to sow in the fresh furrows.

Strange seed that was, for no sooner had the earth covered it than the whole field began to stir and swell as if it were alive, and from every heaving clod glistened blades that were not green grass but sharp bronze and iron, the bare ground quickly bursting forth with a crop of helmets and spears which rose higher every moment, and grew up above shields and clanging mail till every furrow bristled with a rank of armed warriors,

Jason Charming the Dragon, by Salvator Rosa, 1615–1673. Oil on canvas. (The Montreal Museum of Fine Arts, Montreal, Canada.) With Medea's help, Jason sprinkled a magical potion on the dragon's eyes.

to be mowed down by Jason ere the sun sank over the sea. And now Medea's secret counsel served him well, for he took not spear nor sword in hand, but, when the warriors were full grown and stood like bearded corn ripe for the sickle, he pitched amidst them a huge stone, such as might have made a quoit for a giant. The rattle and crash of it was drowned by the yells of the armed men, turning here and there to ask who had cast this missile against them. So hot for fight were they that forthwith they fell blindly upon one another, wrestling together and plying sword and spear on the joints of each other's harness. Thus madly and blindly they fought, some springing up from the ground only to be reaped in death. So, while Jason leant on his spear to watch how these prodigious foes struck down their own brethren, the fight went on till the furrows were filled with blood and the field lay strewn with corpses, laid low as under a hailstorm. And when the sun set, the earth had swallowed up that monstrous brood, where now green grass grew over their bones.

Black were the brows of Æetes as Jason came to demand the Golden Fleece, since he had fulfilled the hard task set him.

"We will speak of that to-morrow," answered the king, turning away sullenly to his halls, while the Grecian Heroes, proud and glad, went back to their ship.

There, as they sat at supper, into the blaze of their fire stole Medea with breathless haste to warn them what was afoot. Her father, she disclosed, was secretly gathering his warriors, and meant to set upon them next morning with overwhelming might. If they would win the Fleece, it must be now or never. She herself would guide Jason to the grove where it hung, and by her spells she could lull its fearsome guardian to sleep. Then he must seize it and fly before the sun rose.

This witch-maiden having already schooled him so well, Jason could not doubt again to do her bidding. His comrades left to unmoor the *Argo* and make all ready for instant flight, he alone let Medea guide him to the sacred shrine. With her had come her young brother Absyrtus; and he too followed, trembling for fear.

At dead of night they entered the gloomy grove of Ares, where at once they heard the blood-curdling hiss of that watchful serpent, whose coils glittered like lightning about the tall tree on which hung the Golden Fleece, turned to silver in the moonlight. Lightly as they trod through the tangled thicket, before they came in sight by flitting moonbeams, the monster had raised his fearsome head and opened his poison-breathing jaws. But Medea stole up to him with a soft, low chant that charmed his ears, and she sprinkled his eyes with a magical potion brewed from honey and herbs, and let its drowsy odour rise through his jaws, till soon this potent drug filled him with sleep. The serpent stretched out his measure-less coils to lie still as any fallen branch, overpowered by the arts of the murmuring enchantress. When his hissing had changed to deathlike silence, Jason stepped warily over the scaly bulk, nor did that fierce guardian stir as he laid hands on the Golden Fleece, and tore it down from

Removing the Golden Fleece. "The fierce guardian did not stir as Jason laid hands on the Golden Fleece and tore it down." From *The Heroes* by Charles Kingsley, 1868, London.

where it had hung since Phrixus nailed it there. "Away!" was now the word, before the grisly serpent should awaken from the spell cast upon him. But as Jason turned exultingly towards his ship, Medea held him back, and her song broke into lamenting.

"Well for thee that canst speed homeward to friends and honour! But woe is me, poor maiden, whom an angry father will slay when he knows how I have helped the stranger against him!"

"No stranger to one for whom thou hast played such a friendly part!" quoth Jason. "Fly with me, Medea, as my bride, without whose aid I might have gone back dishonoured. Thus I shall bear home two treasures for one, and be most envied among the sons of Greece. Speak, wilt thou share my fortune?"

She answered not, but a maiden's silence may be more than speech. So, bearing up the Fleece with one hand, he cast the other around her, and it needed no force to draw away the daughter of Colchis, who might never see her father's land again. Side by side, the pair hastened down to the harbour; and the weeping boy Absyrtus clung to his sister, knowing not where she went.

With the first beam of dawn they came to the *Argo*, where the crew, sitting ready at their oars, hailed the Golden Fleece with a shout of joy to waken all Colchis. Medea and her brother being led on board, and the trophy fastened to their mast, Jason cut the cable by one stroke of his sword, then away went the *Argo* like a horse let loose, soon bounding beyond sight of that eastern shore.

The Hall of Mysteries in the Telesterion, part of the Sacred Enclosure at Eleusis, ancient sanctuary of the Eleusian mysteries. The Telesterion was designed in the fifth century B.C. by Iktinos, architect of the Parthenon. Photographed by Edwin Smith in the 1960s.

Medea

King Æetes was early astir, arming himself and his men to fall upon those presumptuous strangers when they should come to demand the Fleece. But daybreak showed him the *Argo* flying across the sea; and hot was his wrath to learn that she had carried off his daughter and his son along with the chief treasure of Colchis, on which hung his own life. Quickly making ready his fleet, he launched forth to follow with so many ships that they covered the dark water like a flock of seagulls.

The Argonauts, seeing themselves pursued, hoisted every sail and tugged their best at the oars. But now it was ill for that crew that they had lost stout Hercules as well as other strong arms. For all they could do, the Colchian ships gained upon them so fast that one-half of Jason's men had to stand on guard grasping spear and shield, while the other half rowed with all their might.

"On, on!" ever cried Medea, fearing to fall into her father's hands; and when his ship drew so near that she could see his stern face and hear his threatening voice, the cruel witch did a deed from which Jason might know, as he would know to his sorrow, what a fierce and ruthless bride he had stolen away. In spite of the boy's tears and entreaties, she hurled her brother Absyrtus overboard; nay, some say that she had him torn in

The Golden Fleece by Herbert James Draper, 155 × 270 cm, 1904. (Bradford Art Galleries and Museums, England.) In spite of the boy's tears and entreaties, she hurled her brother overboard.

pieces and thrown upon the waves that their father might be delayed by gathering up the dead body for pious burial.

So it was; and thus the *Argo* escaped from mortal foemen, soon to be hidden in a cloud of thunder with which the gods proclaimed their wrath against that hateful crime. Henceforth, for long, Jason's crew wandered as under a curse, abandoned for a time, it would seem, even by Hera's favour, when the king of heaven frowned upon them. They were driven astray by storms, blinded in mists, and tossed on many a strange sea, ere the guilt of innocent blood could be washed away from their ship. Broken and befouled, it came on the rocks of an unknown land; and no man can well tell how and where its crew made their way onward. Some say that Medea had enchantments to drive it over the land as on the sea.

The Argonauts travelled now up a great river and across mountains and deserts, their ship dragged with them, till once more they could launch it in the Mediterranean Sea, repaired and rigged afresh for another voyage. Still trouble and danger were their penance, even when by sacrifices and holy rites they had appeased the gods for the death of Absyrtus. Many strange adventures befell them among the same perilous straits and giant-haunted islands as were afterwards known to the wandering Ulysses; they had to steer past Scylla and Charybdis and the luring Sirens; then but for Medea's crafty spells those stout hearts might never have won home to Greece. They were wrecked on the desert shore of Libya, and once more had to drag their battered *Argo* over its barren sands. Launching again, they came past Crete, to find this island guarded by the giant Talus, whose monstrous body and limbs were of red-hot brass, but for one vulnerable vein in his heel. When the Argonauts would have landed for food and water, from the cliffs he hurled mighty rocks at their vessel, that would have been sunk had they not sheered off in haste. But Medea, boldly going on shore, laid Talus fast asleep by her magical incantations, then wounded his heel of flesh to spill all his life-blood, so that the heat went out of his huge body, and it rolled from the rocks, crashing and splashing into the sea.

So many years had passed, that when at last they saw Iolcos, the band of hopeful youths who followed Jason came back weary and toilworn men, grown old before their time. They were hardly to be known by their friends, as they stepped on shore amid cries of amazement, welcome, and triumph at the sight of the Golden Fleece they brought as proof of their achievement. Pelias had long given them up for dead, never having thought they could come back alive with such a trophy. He himself was now drawing near to death, yet his palsied hands clung to the ill-gotten sceptre, and, for all his promise, he would not yield up the kingdom to Jason. But Medea had wiles deeper than his own. He and his looked askance on the Colchian witch, till she offered by her magic to make him young again, as she did for a ram which, boiled in a caldron with certain herbs, came forth under strange incantations a tender lamb. Thereby she persuaded the daughters of Pelias to do the like with their old father, who thus perished miserably, slain by the hands of his own children. But some tell how Æson, Jason's father, was indeed restored to youth by the Colchian witch, and that he reigned again at Iolcos.

Jason himself had no mind for a kingdom gained by so wicked arts; and it might well be that his heart grew cold to such a cruel wife. Once more wandering from home, he fell in love with Glauce, the daughter of Creon, king of Corinth. He hoped to make Medea content with his second marriage; but not yet did he know the stern-hearted stranger he had taken to his side. Dissembling her hate, the enchantress sent to Glauce a rich wedding robe, steeped in poison, which was the death of that woeful bride, vainly striving to tear the splendid torment from her flesh. Then, in the madness of jealousy, Medea slew her three young sons with her own hand; and when Jason furiously turned from their bodies to take vengeance on the unnatural mother, he saw her for the last time borne away through the air in a chariot drawn by dragons.

So a hero's life on which such bright suns had risen, was to set in dark clouds of affliction. Some say that in his frenzy he killed himself by the corpses of his children and of his murdered bride. But others tell how, as he sat by the seashore beside his good ship *Argo*, thinking sadly on the glorious days when she had borne him to Colchis, the rotten figurehead broke off and crushed him: so his protecting goddess sent death as the best gift to a man whose work was done.

The Fury of Medea, by Eugene Delacroix. Oil on canvas, 260 × 165 cm, 1838. (Musée des Beaux Arts, Lille, France.) Medea murdered Glauce, Jason's new love, and then in a frenzy killed her own sons.

THESEUS

Aethra Gives Theseus the Sandals. "So shall I be like Hercules," Theseus said, "and come more welcome if I bring his sandals." From *The Heroes* by Charles Kingsley, 1868, London.

The Temple of Theseus at Athens. Coloured engraving, 1840. Theseus, King of Athens, was worthy of a temple – he participated in the Calydonian boar hunt, helped defeat the Amazons, and slew the Minotaur.

Ægeus, the old king of Athens, was believed to have no children, so the sons of his brother Pallas, known as the Pallantids, looked to seize the throne on his death. But years ago, Ægeus had made a secret marriage with Æthra, daughter of Pittheus, king of Trœzen, moved thereto by an oracle that also promised him from that union a son destined to rare renown. Yet soon he left poor Æthra, taking leave of her at a huge rock on the seashore which he rolled away to hide beneath it his great sword and his sandals.

"Should the gods grant us a son," he charged her, "let him not know his father till he be strong enough to move this stone; then let him seek me out at Athens, bearing the sword and sandals as tokens."

In due time Æthra bore a son named Theseus, whom she kept in ignorance of his race, and among her own people he passed as being the child of Poseidon, to whom special reverence was paid at this seaport of Argolis. The boy, indeed, grew up so lustily that he might well be thought of more than mortal birth. While he was still a child, Hercules visited Trœzen, who was his kinsman by the mother's side; and the sight of such a famous champion and the tales of his exploits filled young Theseus with longing for the like adventures. While other children shrank from the lion's skin the hero wore, he flew upon it with his little sword, taking this for a lion indeed, when one day Hercules had thrown it off his brawny limbs. All through his youth Theseus kept that hero before him as pattern of what he would be; then in after-life he held it an honour to be friend and companion of Hercules.

Deserted by her husband, the mother's comfort was in a son known as the stoutest and boldest lad in the land, prudent, too, and trustworthy beyond his years. For all that Theseus was loved by Æthra, she did not forget how the time for their parting drew on. When he was full grown, she took him to the rock by the shore and bid him roll it away, as he did with ease, to find beneath it the sword and sandals hidden here by Ægeus. Then first she told him his true father's name, and that he must seek out the king at Athens, taking the sword and sandals as tokens of his birth.

Full of pride to know himself the son of such a king, and of eagerness to see the world, Theseus made light of his old grandfather's counsel that he should go to Athens by sea. Greece in those days had sore trouble from tyrants, robbers, and wild monsters; and the youth's heart was set upon ridding the country of pests such as he might expect to meet on his way to Athens by land.

"So shall I be like Hercules," he told his anxious mother, "and come more welcome to my father if I bring his sandals worn by travel and his sword stained with blood."

The mother sighed, but let him take his way. He would not even choose the easiest road, but went up into the mountains behind Epidaurus on the east coast of Argolis. There he had not gone far, when out of a wood rushed the robber Periphetes, brandishing a huge club and calling on him to stand. Theseus stood firm, sword in hand, and when they closed in hot tussle, that club-bearer for once met his match. The youth nimbly avoided every crushing blow, drove his sword through the robber's heart, then went forward triumphantly bearing the club of Periphetes and his bearskin cloak as trophies.

With this cloak he felt himself like his model Hercules; and before long it served him well, when he came to the isthmus of Corinth, haunted by a wretch named Sinis, of whom men spoke with dread as the

The Acropolis, Athens, photographed by Edwin Smith in the 1960s. Acropolis was the name given to the highest part of cities, where treasure was guarded, and the gods were worshipped.

"pine-bender", for it was his wont to slay what unfortunates fell into his hands after a cruel manner: bending down two pines he would fasten the man between them, and let them spring up to tear his members asunder. But when he would have so dealt with Theseus the young hero felled him to the ground, bound him with his own cords, and let his bones be shot into the air to feed the kites.

Before leaving the isthmus, Theseus turned aside to hunt down a fierce wild sow that ravaged the fields and had been the death of all other hunters. The country people, glad to be rid of this pest, warned him of another foe upon his way. Going from Corinth to Megara, on a narrow ledge of rock above the shore he would pass the giant Sceiron, whose humour was to bid wayfarers wash his feet, and to kick them over into the sea while so obeying him. To hear of such a peril was enough for Theseus, who now would not be persuaded to take any road but this. He went to meet that churlish giant, and, when called on to wash his feet, hurled the great Sceiron over the steep into the sea, to be changed into a rock washed for ever by the waves.

Next he came to Eleusis, where the people, pitying so gallant a youth, would have had him slink past without being seen by their tyrant Cercyon, who, trusting in his mighty bones and sinews, challenged every stranger to wrestle with him, and none had yet come alive out of his clutch. But Theseus was not one to pass by such an adversary. He went up to the palace, ate and drank with the king, and willingly stripped for a struggle in which the insolent Cercyon fell never to rise again; then the citizens, delivered from that oppressor, would have had Theseus stay with them as their king.

But Theseus would not tarry, hastening on to Athens past the den of another monstrous evildoer, to fall in with whom he was all the readier for the warnings given him. This was Procrustes, or the "Stretcher", who would lie in wait for harmless travellers and with friendly words lure them to his dwelling as guests, there to divert himself upon them with a cruel device. He had two beds, one over long, the other too short for a grown man's body. Were the stranger short of stature, this giant's way was to put him into the longer bed and stretch out his limbs to fill it; but if tall, he was laid on the smaller one and his legs were cut down till he fitted that.

"Such a one were well brought to an end by his own tricks," quoth Theseus to himself, when, as his wont was, Procrustes came out offering hospitality to this wayfarer.

The youth, feigning to be deceived, cheerfully turned aside with him, then staggering and gaping as if he were tired out, let himself be led into the torture chamber.

"Friend," chuckled the giant, "you see how it is! This other bed of mine is too short for a youth of your inches; yet can I soon make that shortcoming right."

But as he would have laid Theseus on the shorter bed, suddenly he found himself caught in a grasp of iron, flung off his feet, thrown down

Hippodaemia on her Wedding Day. The marriage of Hippodaemia and King Pirithous was disrupted by the intoxicated Centaur, Eurytion, who rashly abducted the bride. From the west pediment of the Temple of Zeus at Olympia, 468–460 B.C.

and bound for the stranger to hack and hew him with his own axe, and so he came to the miserable death he had wrought on many another.

This was the hero's last exploit on his way to Athens. On the banks of the Cephissus, he next fell in with friendly men, who refreshed him after his toils, washed him clear of blood and dust, and sent him on with good wishes, nor without pious rites and sacrifices to purify him if he had done aught amiss on that adventurous journey.

Yet a deadlier danger than all awaited him when at last he came to his father's home. Ægeus, wellnigh in his dotage, was no longer master at Athens. Treason and rebellion filled the streets of the city, where his nephews the Pallantids took on themselves to rule with insolent pride, while in his palace the old king had fallen under the power of Medea, that wicked witch-woman, who lighted here after flying from Jason at Corinth. By her magic arts she had foreseen the coming of Theseus; and she knew at once who must be the noble youth that now presented himself in the king's hall. It was easy for her to make the feeble old man take this for some secret foe bent on his harm. Then the enchantress mixed poison in a bowl of wine, which she offered the stranger as welcome, whispering to Ægeus that thus they should be surely rid of him.

Hippolytus and Phaedra. Hippolytus, son of Theseus, was falsely accused of dishonour by Phaedra. Theseus afterwards learned the innocence of his son, and Phaedra, in despair, made away with herself. Roman sarcophagus from Solona, first to third century A.D. (Archaeological Museum, Spalato, Italy.)

But before Theseus drank, he drew forth the sword glittering in his father's sight, not so dim but that Ægeus remembered it as his own; and his dull eyes grew bright as he guessed this goodly young man for his long-forgotten son. Coming to himself, he dashed the poisoned drink on the ground; and in a moment father and son were in each other's arms.

The cunning witch-queen might well scowl at their happy meeting. She felt that her power over the doting king was gone; and in her dragon-chariot she fled away from Greece for ever. Theseus, hailed as his father's heir, was soon able to quell the disorders of the kingdom. He drove out of Athens the insolent Pallantids, who already bore themselves as kings; and, young as he was, he showed himself so worthy that all the citizens were content to obey a ruler blessed with such a son to uphold him. The first service he did to his new country was to rid it of the fierce bull of Marathon, the dread of which had long kept the husbandmen from tilling their lands. Many a hunter had sought that monster to his own hurt, before Theseus, setting out alone against it, brought the bull alive from its lair, led it as a show through the streets, and offered it as a sacrifice to the gods that had given him such strength and valour.

Hippolytus was flung out of his chariot and dragged to his death by his frightened horses who bolted at the sight of a sea monster sent by Poseidon. Engraving from an illustrated edition of *Metamorphoses* by Ovid, published in 1683 in Amsterdam.

Ere long, the heir of Ægeus had the chance to do a greater deed for Athens, a deed never to be forgotten in song and history. Years before, on Athenian ground had been treacherously slain Androgeos, son of the mighty Minos, king of Crete. Some say that this crime sprang from jealousy, since the Cretan prince had beaten the athletes of the country in their own games. The father, to avenge his blood, had made war on Athens, to which he granted peace at the price of a sore tribute. Every nine years, seven of its finest youths and fairest maidens must be sent to Crete, there to be delivered to the Minotaur, a fearsome creature, half-beast and

Theseus in the Labyrinth, by E. Burne-Jones. Design for a tile, 1862. Ariadne gave Theseus a clue of thread to unwind on his way through the labyrinth, that he might retrace his steps.

Daedalus showing the wooden cow to Pasiphae, wife of King Minos. Fresco at the Casa dei Vetti, Pompeii, first century A.D. Daedalus was a skilled craftsman and inventor, who designed the labyrinth at Cnossus, to house the bull-child of Queen Pasiphae.

half-man, by which they were savagely devoured. Now, for the third time, this tribute had to be paid, the victims chosen by lot among the noblest families of the city. But when it came to drawing lots, Theseus stood forth to offer himself freely.

"The lot falls first on me, as son of your king!" he declared. "I will head the tribute band, and let the Minotaur taste my sword first of all, that has slain as fierce monsters."

His generous devotion filled the citizens with gratitude, but the old king was loath to risk his only son on such a perilous chance. In vain he begged Theseus to hold back; the hero's spirit was keen and steadfast as his sword. So on the appointed day, he embarked for Crete among the tale of luckless youths and maidens, followed by the prayers of their woeful parents. His own father, hardly hoping to see him again, made him promise one thing. The ship that bore this doomed band was wafted by black sails in sign of mourning; but if it should be their lot to come back safe, they were to hoist a white sail, that not an hour should be lost in showing good news to those on the watch for their return.

With winds but too fair for so forlorn an errand, the ship came safe to the city of Minos. There he kept the Minotaur in his famous labyrinth, a maze of winding passages in the rock, made for him by Dædalus, that cunning artificer of old, who, when he had served the Cretan king long and well, offended him to such wrath, that with his young son Icarus he had needs fly away to Sicily. The crafty Dædalus knew how to fit wings to their shoulders, fastened by wax; and thus they sped over the sea, the father coming safe to land, but when heedless Icarus flew too near the sun, the wax melted, and, losing his wings, he fell into a sea thenceforth called the Icarian, after his name. His body was wafted far away over the waves, to be in time drawn ashore by Hercules, who gave it burial on an island also named from him, Icaria.

Minos might well be proud to see the prince of Athens offer himself to glut his revenge; yet even his stern heart took pity on this noble youth, so boldly claiming as a right to be first to face the ravenous monster.

"Bethink thee, ere it be too late," he warned Theseus. "Naked and alone, thou must seek out the Minotaur, that has torn in pieces every victim turned into its haunt. And even couldst thou escape such an enemy, no stranger, venturing within the labyrinth, has ever been able to find his way out of its dark secrets."

"So be it, if so it must be!" answered Theseus; and that night was set for his dreadful ordeal.

But not in vain had the hero, at the bidding of an oracle, invoked for his enterprise the protection of Aphrodite, goddess of love. One friend he had in Crete, before ever a word passed between them. Ariadne, daughter of King Minos, looked with kind eyes on this gallant stranger, and her heart was hot to save him from so miserable death. Seeking him out by stealth, she whispered good cheer and counsel in his ear, giving him a clue of thread which he should unroll as he passed on into the labyrinth's windings, then, his task done, he might follow that helpful clue till it brought him back to the free air. Moreover, she put into his hand a magic sword, with which, and with none other, the Minotaur might be slain. And, if he came out safe, she made him promise to carry her away from her father's anger, as Theseus willingly agreed, when the very favour of so bright eyes seemed a charm to bring him safe through all dangers.

Thus equipped, he took his way alone into the mouth of the labyrinth, leaving the youths and maidens, his comrades, to await what should befall him. With tearful eyes they saw him swallowed up in the darkness, and heard his steps die away within. Then all was silence, till there burst forth an awful roar echoing through those hollow windings, to show how the Minotaur was aware of his foe. The time seemed long while fearfully they stood listening to a distant din of bellowing and clattering and gnashing. Again, all fell silent; and, quaking at the knees, his companions hardly hoped to see their leader come back from that chill gloom that in turn should be their own grave. But what was their joy at last to catch his voice raised in triumph, then he strode forth into the starlight, his sword dripping with blood!

The hero threw himself on Ariadne's neck to thank her for the aid without which he would never have overcome that monster, nor made his way out of its darksome lair. But she bid him lose no moment in hastening beyond the power of her father and all his men. Taking Ariadne with

The Fall of Icarus, by Thomas Fedrianus, sixteenth century. (Palazzo Vecchio, Florence, Italy.) Forgetting his father's warning, Icarus flew too near the sun, which melted his wings of wax.

Theseus Kills the Minotaur with a magic sword provided by Ariadne. Roman floor mosaic, first century A.D., from the House of Labyrinth, Pompeii. (National Archaeological Museum, Naples, Italy.)

Ariadne on the Island of Naxos, deserted by Theseus, who had dreamt that she would never marry a mortal. By G.F. Watts, oil on canvas, 75 × 94 cm, 1875. (Guildhall Art Gallery, London.)

them, the Athenians got on board their vessel, and had hoisted sail before Minos awoke to see them already far at sea.

And now the pair who had loved each other at first sight would fain have been wedded; but their love went amiss. For Theseus became warned in a dream that his Ariadne was destined as the bride of no mortal man, but of a god. So he hardened his heart to put her ashore on the island of Naxos, and there left her asleep by the strand, sailing away without a word of farewell.

Theseus held on his course with a heavy heart, the joy of victory all overcast for him by Ariadne's loss. And in that sorrow he forgot his father's charge to hoist a white sail if he should come back safe. Day after day, when the ship might be expected, old Ægeus sat upon a high point, straining his weak eyes on watch for her return. At last she came in sight, and lo! the sails were black as death. The king gave up his son for lost. With a cry of despair he flung himself over a cliff into the waves, still known by his name as the Ægean Sea.

So mournful news met Theseus when he sailed into the harbour in triumph, all Athens pressing down to learn how it had fared with him.

With thanksgiving to the gods for their speeding, he had to mingle the funeral rites of his father; and never could the son pardon himself that fatal forgetfulness that made him king of Athens.

THE TRAGEDIES OF THEBES

Cadmus

It is told of Cadmus, the Tyrian, that he first taught the use of letters to Greece. And a strange errand it was that brought this stranger from his home beyond the sea.

His father, king Agenor, had one young daughter, Europa, on whom fell the eyes of Zeus, and he plotted to bear her away to be his own. As Europa was sporting with her companions on the seashore, the god appeared to her in the shape of a milk-white bull, so gentle and goodly that she fell to stroking it and decking its head with flowers, while it licked her neck. As it lay down on the grass, the playful girl made bold to mount

The Rape of Europa. Daughter of King Agenor of Tyre, Europa was stolen away by a milk-white bull. Fresco from Pompeii, Italy, first century A.D. (Archaeological Museum, Naples, Italy.)

its broad back. But she screamed with fright when at once it leapt to its feet, and galloped away with her like a spirited courser and plunged with her into the sea. Heedless of her cries, it bore her across the waves.

All night the bull swam swift and strong as a galley, then at daylight set Europa on an island, which indeed was Crete. There the bull vanished, Zeus taking his own godlike form to tell her how he had done this for love.

But the king of Tyre never ceased to mourn his lost daughter. With a few faithful servants Cadmus crossed the sea, and came into Greece; but there he could still hear no news of his sister, so that at last he lost all hope to find her alive. Without her he might not see his father's face, and he knew not where to turn for a home. Coming to the renowned Delphic oracle of Apollo, he sought its counsel, and was bidden to follow a cow he would find feeding alone in a meadow hard by: where the cow first lay down he should build a city and call its name Thebes.

He soon found the cow, that walked on before him, leading him and his men many a league through fields and hills, into a land of mountains and plains which came to be called Bœotia. There at last the cow, lowing to the sky, laid itself upon the grass as token for Cadmus that his long wandering was at an end. Thankfully he fell down to kiss the strange earth a god seemed to give him for his own.

But the place had a fearsome lord with whom he must reckon. Proposing to offer sacrifice to Pallas-Athene, that she might be favourable

The Rape of Europa, by Riccardo Tommasi Feroni. Oil on canvas, 120 × 140 cm, 1975. Zeus, in the form of a bull, swam to Crete with Europa on his back.

Cadmus Slays the Dragon. "Blood gushed from the dragon's breast to mingle with the foam of its fury." From an illuminated edition of *Metamorphoses* by Ovid, late fifteenth century.

to him, he sent his servants to draw water from a stream which rushed out of a dark cave, its mouth hidden in a thick grove of mossy oaks never touched by the axe. The men entered the grove, but came not back; and from within he heard a sound of hissing, and saw wreaths of foul smoke spreading among the trees. He bounded forward to find his servants lying dead before the cave, scorched by the breath of a huge dragon that stretched towards him its three fiery heads, each bristling with three rows of teeth through which it breathed poisonous fumes, its eyes shining like fire, and its red crests glowing in the shadow of the cave mouth, as it pushed out its long neck to lick the bodies of the slain. Cadmus snatched up a rock to hurl at the monster but it bounced back without doing any harm.

Undaunted, the hero flung his spear so straight and strong that black blood gushed from the dragon's breast to mingle with the foam of its fury. Now it uncoiled all its monstrous length, and issuing from the cave, reared its horrid heads like trees to fall upon the man who dared to face its wounded rage. But Cadmus held his ground, smiting with all his might at the fiery jaws, till he drove his sword through one poison-swollen throat to nail it to an oak trunk. The monster twisted its necks and lashed its tail so as to bend the thick tree double, but the roots held firm, and the sword stuck fast; so there it writhed helplessly while its fiery breath was quenched by its own blood.

Cadmus Sows the Dragon's Teeth. "Forthwith, the gound began to heave and swell and bristle with spear points." From an illuminated edition of *Metamorphoses* by Ovid, late fifteenth century.

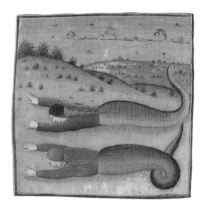

Cadmus and his Wife Turn into Serpents.
Bowed, tired and old, they had prayed
to be serpents rather than mortals.
From an illuminated edition of
Metamorphoses by Ovid, late fifteenth
century.

All unhurt, Cadmus stood over the dead body, when he was aware of Pallas at his side, come down from Olympus to found a city that should grow great under her ægis. "Sow the dragon's teeth in the earth," she bid him. "From them will spring up a race of warlike men to do thy will."

Much wondering at such counsel, Cadmus did not disobey. He dug deep furrows with his sword; he plucked out the dead dragon's teeth; he sowed them in the earth drenched by its gore. Forthwith the ground began to heave and swell and bristle with spear points; then quickly there sprang up a crop of armed men, their weapons clashing together like corn beaten by the wind.

No sooner were the new-born warriors full grown out of the furrows, than they fell on each other in their lust for battle. So fiercely they fought that, before the sun was set, all but five had fallen dead. These five, weary with bloodshed, dropped their weapons and offered themselves to serve Cadmus in place of his followers slain by the dragon.

With their aid he built here the citadel that came to be called Thebes. The new city throve, yet its first lord had to suffer from foes, both in heaven and on earth. The dragon-serpent slain by him was sacred to the gods Ares, who long bore ill will to Cadmus for its death. A curse rested on his house. His children and his children's children came to evil ends, among them Ino, who drowned herself after her husband in madness killed their son, and Semele, consumed by the fierce glory of Zeus, when she became the mother of Dionysus.

Cadmus himself, they say, was dethroned by his own grandson Pentheus. In his old age, the many-woed king had again to go forth homeless, yet not alone, for with him went his faithful wife Harmonia. They wandered into the wild northern forests, till this once dauntless hero, bowed down by infirmities and burdened with the curse of that dragon's blood, was fain to murmur—

"If a serpent be so dear to the gods, would I were a serpent rather than a man!" At once he sank upon his breast, his skin turning to scales and his limbs to speckled coils. As Harmonia saw how her husband was transformed, she prayed that she too might become a serpent; and her prayer likewise was answered. There they dwell still among the rocky woods, hurting no man, nor hiding from the sight of men who were once their fellows.

Niobe

Thebes, thus founded in bloodshed, had a long history written in letters of blood by the hate of rival gods. It was the fate of Pentheus to be torn in pieces by the women of his house, his own mother their leader, because he frowned on their wild worship of Dionysus.

Another queen who worshipped the wine-god was Dirce, wife of the usurper Lycus. The daughter of the rightful king was Antiope, beloved by Zeus, to whom she bore two sons, Amphion and Zethus.

Niobe was turned into a stone on
Mount Sipylus in Lydia, which
during the summer always shed tears.

Niobe's Children are Slain by Apollo and Artemis. Engraving from an illustrated edition of *Metamorphoses* by Ovid, published in 1683 in Amsterdam.

Amphion became king at Thebes, which he walled about through the power of music, being so skilled to play on a lyre given him by Hermes, that at its enchanting sound the very stones were drawn to move as he bade them. But on his children, too, fell a curse of wrath and woe.

Amphion had married Niobe, daughter of the doomed Tantalus, who was himself a son of Zeus. She bore seven noble sons and seven fair daughters; then, too proud of this goodly brood, she made bold to exult over Leto, as mother of twins and no more. But these twins were the divine Apollo and Artemis, on whom their despised mother called to avenge her against that presumptuous queen.

Wrapt in dark storm-clouds, brother and sister flew to overlook

Oedipus and the Sphinx, by Charles Ricketts. Drawing, 1891. (The Guildhall Museum, Carlisle, England.) Furious that Oedipus could answer its riddle, the Sphinx flew away, never to be seen again.

Thebes, where on an arena outside the walls, the seven sons of Niobe were exercising themselves in chariot racing, wrestling, and other sports. They had no warning unless the clank of the god's quiver, before the eldest was pierced to the heart by an arrow from the sky, and fell without a groan among the feet of his horses. The second turned his chariot to fly, but that did not avail him, struck by Apollo's unerring aim. So, also, it went with the third and fourth and the fifth and sixth sons. The youngest only remained, a long-haired, fair-faced stripling, who, guessing how he had to do with an angry god, threw himself on his knees to beg for mercy, but the fatal point was already winging to his breast.

At the news of this sudden slaughter, Amphion stabbed himself for despair. Niobe, gathering her scared daughters about her, as chickens under the wings of a bird, hurried out to the field on which her seven boys were stretched lifeless around the altar of Leto. At the sight of them, rage spoke louder than grief, and raising her head against the gods who had so avenged their mother, she cried bitterly—

"Triumph, cruel Leto; but even now my offspring surpasses thine!"

For answer twanged the bow of Artemis, and the eldest daughter fell as she stood tearing her hair over her slain brothers. One by one, all the daughters were shot down, till only the youngest in terror hung to her mother, whose pride now gave way.

"Spare me but one, the last of so many!"

As she spoke, the last shaft of pitiless Artemis reached the child on the mother's bosom. Without a wound, Niobe herself sank as dead, her heart broken, her limbs motionless, her eyes staring, the blood gone from her face, where only her tears did not cease to flow. Sorrow had turned her to stone. For ever, they say, as the hot rays of the sun and the cold moonbeams pour down by turns on that stone image, it weeps for the children of whom Niobe had boasted against the jealous gods.

Œdipus

Among all the descendents of Cadmus, the most famous and the most unhappy was Oedipus, son of Laius, doomed by an oracle to be the death of his own father and the husband of his mother. Forewarned of such a fate, when his queen Jocasta bore a boy, Laius had Oedipus cast out on Mount Cithæron. But the goatherd charged with this cruel errand took pity on the wailing infant, and gave it to another herd, who took it to his master Polybus, king of Corinth. By him the boy was kindly received, and brought up under the name of Œdipus. Meanwhile Laius and Jocasta believed themselves to live childless, and thus hoped to cheat the oracle.

Polybus and his childless wife Merope adopted the outcast boy as their own son; then, as years went on, few at Corinth remembered how he was not so in truth. Œdipus grew to manhood never doubting but that these foster-parents were his father and mother, till one day, at a feast, some drunken fellow mocked at him for a baseborn foundling. In wrathful concern he sought to know from Merope whose son he truly was. She tried to put him off, yet could not deny that he was a stranger by birth. The dismayed youth turned to Polybus, who also gave him doubtful answers, bidding him ask no more, since it would be a woeful misfortune if ever he came to know his real parents.

But these hints only made Œdipus more eager to learn the truth, and he bethought himself of Apollo's oracle. Leaving Corinth secretly, he travelled on foot to Delphi, where the priestess vouchsafed no plain answer to his question, but only this fearful warning—

"Shun thy father, ill-omened youth! Shouldst thou meet with him, he will fall by thy hand; then, wedding thine own mother, thou wilt leave a race destined to fresh crimes and woe."

Œdipus turned away with a shudder. Now he believed himself to understand why Polybus and Merope had made a mystery of his birth. Fearing affliction for them, who loved him well, he vowed never to go back to Corinth, but to seek some distant land, where, if madness came upon his mind to drive him to such wicked deeds, he might be far from the parents he took for threatened by so dire a curse.

From Delphi he was making towards Bœotia, when in a narrow

The Tholos at Delphi, *c.* 490 B.C. Delphi, in central Greece, contained the most ancient and influential oracle, consulted on all important issues. The presiding deity was Apollo, god of prophecy.

93

Sphinx, "The Strangling One", was a she-monster, strange and mysterious, with a lion's body and human head. She is said to have proposed a riddle to the Thebans, and to have murdered all who were unable to guess it. Stone statue. (Archaeological Museum, Athens.)

hollow way where three roads met, he came upon an old man in a chariot, before which ran an arrogant servant bidding all stand aside to let it pass. Œdipus, used to bid rather than to be bidden, answered the man hotly, and felled him to the ground; then his master flung a javelin at this presumptuous youth. With his staff Œdipus struck back, overturned the old man from the chariot, and left him dead by the roadside. In the pride of victory Œdipus went his way, ignorant that the proud lord he had slain in a chance quarrel was no other than his own father, Laius.

Wandering from city to city, Œdipus reached Thebes, to find it all in mourning not only for the death of its king, but from the dread of a monster that haunted the rocky heights beyond the wall. This was the Sphinx, which men took to be a sister of Cerberus, that three-headed hound of Hades. To anyone coming near it, the creature put a riddle, which if he failed to answer, it devoured him on the spot. Till some man should have guessed its riddle, the Sphinx would not be gone; and so long as it brooded over the city, blight and famine wasted the fields around. One or another Theban daily met death in setting his wit against this monster's, and its last victim had been a son of Creon, Jocasta's brother, who for a time ruled the kingless land. Seeing himself unable to get rid of the Sphinx, Creon proclaimed that whoever could answer its riddle, were he the poorest stranger, should have as reward the kingdom of Thebes, with all the dead king's treasures, and the hand of his widow, the Queen Jocasta, in marriage.

As Œdipus entered the city, a herald went through the streets to make this proclamation, that set the friendless youth pricking up his ears. Life seemed not dear to him; all he desired was to escape that destiny of crime threatened by the oracle. At once he presented himself before Creon, declaring that he was not afraid to answer the Sphinx.

They led him outside the walls to the stony wilderness it haunted, strewn with the bones of those who had failed to guess its riddle. Here he must seek out the creature alone, for its very voice made men tremble. Soon was he aware of it perched on a rock, a most grisly monster, with the body of a lion, the wings of an eagle, and the head of a woman. But Œdipus, caring little whether he lived or died, shrank not from its appalling looks.

"Put thy riddle!" he cried; and the Sphinx croaked back—

"What creature alone changes the number of its feet? In the morning it goes on four feet, at midday on two, in the evening on three feet. And with the fewest feet, it has ever the greatest strength and swiftness."

Fixing her cruel eyes on the youth, she frowned to see him not at a loss,—nay, he smiled in her stony face, answering forthwith—

"The riddle is easy. It is man that in childhood goes on all-fours, then walks firmly on two feet, and in his old age must lean upon a staff."

Furious to hear her riddle guessed for the first time, the Sphinx gave a shrill scream, flapped her gloomy wings, and vanished among the rocks, never more to be seen at Thebes. With shouts of joy the watching citizens poured out to greet that ready-witted youth that had delivered them from such a scourge. They hailed him as their king; and he was married to the widowed Jocasta.

Years, then, he reigned at Thebes in peace and prosperity, gladly obeyed by the people, who took this young stranger for a favourite of the gods. He loved his wife Jocasta, older than himself as she was; and they had four children, the twin-sons Eteocles and Polynices, and two daughters, Antigone and Ismene. But when these were grown to full age, the fortune of the land seemed to change. For now a sore plague fell upon it, so that the people cried for help to their king, who sent to Delphi his brother-in-law, Creon, to ask of the Delphic oracle how the pestilence might be stayed.

The answer was that it came as punishment for the unatoned blood of Laius. Now, for the first time, Œdipus set on foot enquiries as to his predecessor's death. Vowing to do justice on the criminal, whoever this might prove to be, he consulted Tiresias the seer, struck with blindness in his youth because he had spied upon the goddess Athene. Though the blind seer was loath to tell what Œdipus sought to know, he spoke.

"Hear then, oh king, if thou must learn the truth. Thou thyself art the man that slew Laius in the hollow way to Delphi. For thy sake, and no other, this curse is come upon the city."

Now with a start Œdipus remembered that old lord in the chariot whom he had slain in quarrel as he came from Delphi. But his wife mocked at the seer's wisdom.

"Even the god's oracle may speak falsely," she said, "for Laius was warned at Delphi that he should fall by the hand of his own son, who, moreover, should marry his mother. Yet we never had but one child, and he was thrown out to die on Mount Cithæron when not three days old, that thus our house should escape so dark a doom."

Among the bystanders chanced to be that goatherd charged long ago with the child's death; and him Jocasta called to confirm her words. But the old man fell on his knees, confessing how he had not had the heart to leave a helpless babe to be torn by wolves and eagles, but had given it alive to a servant of the king of Corinth.

Jocasta raised a cry, for she knew her husband passed for a son of that king, and she began to guess the truth that he and no other had unwittingly fulfilled the oracle by slaying his own father and wedding his mother. While he stood aghast, she fled to her chamber, barring herself in with her unspeakable woe. When the door was broken open, she had hanged herself with her girdle rather than look again upon the husband who was no other than her son.

"Thy sorrows are ended; but for me death were too light a punishment!" he wept upon her dead body. And with the buckle of Jocasta's girdle he bored out the sight of both his eyes, so that night came upon him at noonday.

A blind old man, his hair grown suddenly grey, Œdipus groped his

The Plague of Thebes (following page), by Charles François Jalabeat, 1819–1901. Oil on canvas. (Musée des Beaux Arts, Marseilles, France.) Antigone was a noble and defiant maiden, with a truly heroic attachment to her father and brothers. When her father, Oedipus, had put out his eyes in anger and grief, and was obliged to quit Thebes, Antigone accompanied him into exile. She remained with him until he found peace in death at Colonos.

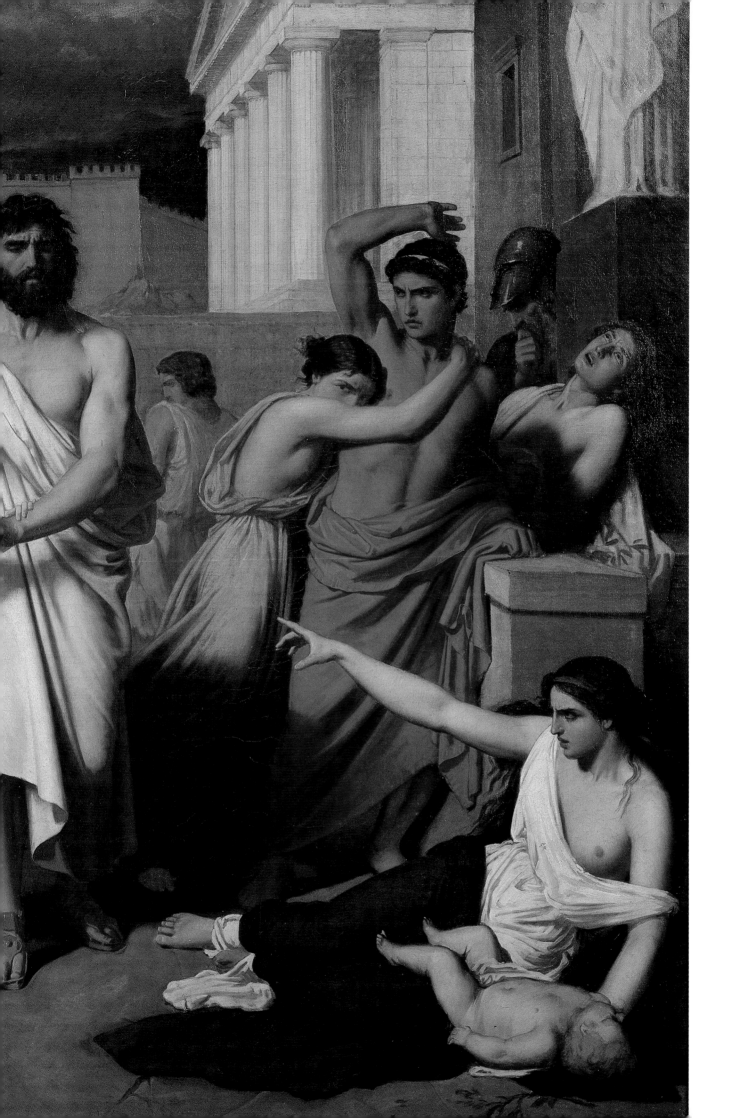

way out of the palace, poorly dressed as he had entered it a travel-worn youth; and leaning on the staff with which he had been the death of his father. His people turned away from him shuddering. His own sons held aloof. Only his daughters, Antigone and Ismene, followed him tearfully, begging him to stay.

Antigone vowed that she would never desert her father, and with him she wandered away from her birthplace. Led by her, he went from city to city as a blind beggar, till they came to Athens, where Theseus was king. He gave the exiles refuge in a temple at Colonos. In this sanctuary Œdipus lived on for some years, poor and sorrowful, pitied by his neighbours as a victim of fate, and gently tended by Antigone till death came to end his strange misfortunes.

The Seven against Thebes

After the death of her old father, Antigone went back to Thebes, where she found her twin-brothers at hot strife. Eteocles and Polynices had agreed to share the kingdom between them, ruling year about. By and by Eteocles, in his turn of office, drove his brother from the city, where he henceforth reigned alone.

Thus exiled, Polynices sought refuge at Argos, hoping for the help of its king, Adrastus.

Adrastus warmly took up the cause of Polynices against Eteocles, and called on kinsmen and allies to gather an army for restoring him to his kingdom. Seven were the captains of that host—Adrastus, his brothers Hippomedon and Parthenopæus, his nephew Capaneus, his brother-in-

The Oath of the Seven Chiefs. Illustration from designs by Flaxman and others, from *Stories From the Greek Tragedians*, by A.J. Church, 1880, London. With help from Argos, Polynices waged war on his Uncle Creon in an ill-fated effort to reclaim the throne of Thebes.

law Amphiaraus, Tydeus, and Polynices himself, they who came to be famed as the Seven against Thebes.

One only of these heroes had hung back from the enterprise—Amphiaraus, renowned both as warrior and as seer. Divining by his art that only one of the Seven would come back alive from Thebes, Amphiaraus, to escape the King's importunities, hid himself in a secret place known only to his wife Eriphyle. The son of Jocasta had brought from Thebes an ancestral treasure, no other than that fatal necklace made by Hephæstus for Harmonia, wife of Cadmus. With this dazzling gaud he bribed Eriphyle to disclose her husband's hiding-place and to persuade him to go against Thebes. Unwilling at heart, Amphiaraus then joined the host; but so resentful was he of his wife's treacherous vanity that, before setting out, he made his son Alcmæon swear to kill Eriphyle, if the father should not come back alive.

In sight of Thebes, the allied host encamped on Mount Cithæron; and Tydeus went forward as a herald to demand that Polynices should be received into his kingdom. Eteocles sent him back with an insolent answer of defiance, for the city, full of armed men, was fortified by a high wall with seven gates, behind which the usurper felt sure of his defence. Yet to hearten the citizens, he called on the blind soothsayer, Tiresias, who gave out a dark foreboding—

"Thebes stands in dire peril, to be averted only by the youngest son of its royal house; his life alone is the sacrifice that, freely offered, can save the city from destruction."

Thebes in Boetia, the "land of mountains and plains", where Cadmus was led by a bull to the site on which was founded the city of Thebes. Coloured engraving, 1828.

At this utterance, none was more dismayed than Creon, Jocasta's brother, for he thought how his darling son Menœceus was the youngest of the fated family. He proposed, then, to send him off to Delphi, there to be kept safe under sanctuary of Apollo. But the brave stripling had at once devoted his life to his native city. The oracle no sooner heard, Menœceus hastened to the highest tower of the walls, and hurled himself over among the assailants.

And that sacrifice seemed to avail for the safety of Thebes. Each of the seven heroes stormed at a different gate; but all were driven back by the defenders, who, sallying out, spread death and rout among their enemy. So many brave warriors fell, that when once more the Argive host came on, Eteocles sent a herald to propose that the quarrel should forthwith be settled by single combat between him and Polynices.

Thus it was agreed: the brothers met outside the walls, and fought before the two armies. They clashed together like boars; they broke their spears on one another's shields; they took to their swords, closing in desperate thirst for a brother's blood that poured out from all the joints of their armour, till both sank dying on the field.

Both sides now claiming the victory, in their dispute they fell to fighting with more fury than ever. Again the invaders were routed, and fled, all their leaders, save Adrastus, having fallen, as Amphiaraus had foretold. Yet the Thebans, too, suffered such loss that a battle won so dearly came to be known as a Cadmean victory.

Antigone

The sons of Œdipus being no more, Creon again took over the kingdom, as he had done after the death of Laius. His first order was that, to mark the infamy of Polynices in warring against his mother's city, his body, and those of his allies, should lie unburied, a prey to dogs and vultures. So, while they bore Eteocles to the tomb with royal pomp, his brother's corpse was left to be parched by the sun and drenched by the dew, a guard set over it night and day.

But Antigone, faithful to her brother as to her father, had stood beside the dying Polynices; and with his last breath he had made her promise to do for him those funeral rites without which his soul might not rest in peace. Alone, in the moonlit night, Antigone stole forth to the field strewn with corpses, among which she searched out her brother's. Washing it with tears, she strove to drag it away; but her strength failed her, and she must make haste, not to be seen by the watchmen. All she could do was softly and silently to sprinkle the body with dust; but that seemed enough to save it from miserable wandering on the bank of Styx.

In the morning, one of the guards came in fear to tell Creon that, for all their watchfulness, Polynices' body had through the night been lightly covered with earth, by whose hands they knew not. Creon wrathfully bid them uncover it, and keep better watch.

Through the day sprang up a mighty whirlwind, filling the air with dust. Antigone again ventured out, to find, as she feared, that her brother's body had been stripped of its thin coat of earth. Again, now in broad daylight, she was trying to cover it, when the guard seized her and brought her, bound, before Creon, who stormed like a tyrant on learning by whom he had been thus defied.

"Rash girl!" he cried, "know'st thou not the law made but yesterday?"

"I know a higher law that is neither of yesterday nor to-day," she answered with unshrinking eye, "the eternal law of pity, that forbids me to leave the dead son of my mother unburied."

Enraged by her boldness, Creon gave command that she should be walled up in a cave and there left to die. Then came Creon's son Hæmon, who was betrothed to Antigone, and loved her more than his life. Reverently addressing his father, he besought him to consider how all men would cry shame on him for such cruelty.

"Would the boy teach me wisdom?" his furious father cut him short. "I see how love for that traitress blinds thee; but thou shalt not have my foe for a bride."

When Antigone had been borne off to her doom, there came another to bend Creon's stubborn will. This was the blind Tiresias, whose inner vision warned him of fresh calamities for Thebes, polluted through the innocent fate of Antigone and the sacrilegious exposure of Polynices. The gods were wroth, he declared, at the wrong thus done to a king's children.

Decorated grave column, from an Athenian vase, *c*. 550 B.C. The Greeks regarded the burial of the dead as one of their most sacred duties. Its neglect involved an offence against the gods and the dead, for a soul would not rest until its body was buried.

"Before the sun sets, thou shalt pay for double impiety—yea, two corpses for one! Their blood be on thy head! Lead me far from him who defies the gods!" So solemn had been his warning, that Creon, left alone, began to falter in his ruthless purpose. He called the elders of the city into council, and of them deigned at last to ask what he should do.

"Bury the body of Polynices, and set Antigone free from her living tomb!" they answered with one voice.

Since all men were against him, Creon sullenly gave way. He ordered Polynices to be honourably buried beside his brother, and went himself to the cave in which Antigone had been walled up. Hæmon, her lover, ran on first of the crowd bearing axes and bars to set her free; then peering through a cleft, he uttered a lamentable cry for what he saw within. Too late the wall was broken down, letting all see how the noble Antigone had strangled herself with her veil twisted into a noose. Hæmon in speechless despair drew his sword, and, before the father could hold his hand, had fallen upon it over the body of his beloved one.

When his mother, Creon's queen, heard what had befallen, she, too, killed herself for grief; thus Tiresias spoke truly that, before the sun set, the king's house should pay two corpses for one. All the city was one cry of mourning, amid which the bereaved Creon hardened his heart, and in his gloomy rage, once more forbade the burial of those slain foes about the city. But again the widowed and childless king had to bend his obstinate will. Adrastus, by the swiftness of his horse, had escaped to Athens, and help from its king, Theseus. With a strong army he marched to Thebes, summoning Creon to let the dead be buried, that their spirits should have rest. The Thebans were in no heart for further fighting; and their tyrant had nothing for it but to consent. The fallen followers of those seven heroes were heaped into seven piles, to be solemnly burned on the field, with due rites. Over the ashes, Theseus built a temple to Nemesis, genius of Retribution; then he withdrew with his allies; and for a time Thebes had peace to lament its evil destiny.

The Delphic Oracle was consulted on all important matters. The Pythia or priestess took her seat on a tripod placed above a chasm in the ground from which arose intoxicating vapours.

The Fatal Heirlooms

Thebes was still to suffer from the bane laid on its kingly house, that spread far beyond its own soil. Polynices had left a son, Thersander, to grow up in exile at Argos. When years had passed, he and other sons of the heroes slain before Thebes began to hatch revenge upon the hated city, and made against it a new war known as that of the Epigoni, or offspring of the Seven.

Of those Seven, Adrastus was still alive, but too old to lead the army. He sought counsel of the oracle at Delphi, that bid choose as chief Alcmæon, son of Amphiaraus, the seer. But Alcmæon shrank from this honour put upon him, while also the oracle reminded him how he had pledged himself to revenge upon his mother Eriphyle the death of his father, betrayed by her to death for the bribe of that fatal necklace, but his dreadful vow was still unfulfilled. Eriphyle had some strange spell to throw over the will of her son, as of her husband. And, as against her husband, so she could be bribed to persuade her son. Thersander had one more Cadmean heirloom to bestow, the rich veil which was another wedding gift of Aphrodite to Harmonia. With this he bought from Eriphyle that she should win over her son to lead the Epigoni.

Alcmæon, then, consented to be their chief, putting off his dark purpose to slay that bewitching mother. He marched to Thebes, where this time the war went for its invaders. The Thebans came out to meet them, but were driven back with the loss of their leader Laodamas, son of Eteocles. The blind Tiresias, now over a hundred years old, gave forth the worst auguries. He bid his fellow citizens send out a herald to propose terms of peace, and under this pretence, to fly from their walls by night. So they did, escaping to seek new homes elsewhere. Thersander entered in triumph the abandoned city, where now he ruled as the last heir of Cadmus, and lived to fall in the great war against Troy.

His fate was happy beside that of Alcmæon, who went back victorious, brooding over the secret vow to slay his mother. To this fell duty, he believed himself urged by the oracle; and it steeled his heart when he came to learn how she had been bribed by the veil of Aphrodite to send him forth in arms. He slew her with his own hand, thus at last performing the long-deferred pledge to his father. But no more could he live in the home made horrible to him. He left Argos and wandered forth alone, taking with him those crime-inspiring gifts.

Then, wherever he went, the gods frowned on him as profaned by his

Apollo, Athene and the Seven Muses. These two divinities, together with the seven Muses, inspired men to produce works of art and craft. Sarcophagus relief, first to second century A.D. (Woburn Abbey, Bedfordshire, England.)

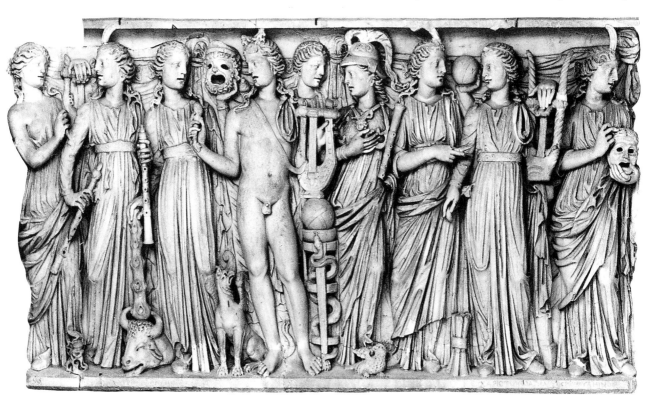

mother's blood, and he was haunted by the Furies into restless madness. In time he seemed to be at peace in a city of Arcadia, whose king Phegeus did purifying rites to cleanse him from his guilt, and gave him in marriage his own daughter Arsinoe. But though his madness had left him, the curse he bore from place to place fell upon the land that thus granted Alcmæon asylum. It was blighted by famine, through his pollution of it; so said the oracle, declaring that this exile could find rest only on ground which should have arisen since he took his mother's life.

Once more he wandered into the world, leaving with Arsinoe those fatal gifts. After long search, he found at the mouth of the river Achelous an island newly sprung above the water, unseen by the sun when he raised his hand against Eriphyle. Here he fixed himself, and seemed now to be free from his curse.

Yet fresh troubles came with relief from the Furies' scourge. Forgetting his wife Arsinoe, he married Callirrhoe, daughter of the river-god Achelous, and she bore him two sons, Acarnan and Amphoterus. They might have lived happily but for Callirrhoe hearing of the famous necklace and veil he had left with Arsinoe, which she coveted so as to give her husband no peace till they should be her own.

Driven by her importunity, Alcmæon went back to Arsinoe, and demanded those fatal gifts on pretence of offering them to Apollo at Delphi, as a sacrifice by which he might be purged of the madness that, as he feigned, alone kept him apart from her. Arsinoe readily gave up her treasures, which he was for carrying off to his new home. But a disloyal servant betrayed to her father how his master had another wife, to be decked with the gifts of Aphrodite. Arsinoe's two brothers followed Alcmæon, slew him taken at unawares, and brought back the necklace and the veil to their sister. She, who loved her false husband still, gave them such bitter thanks for that service, that her also they sent to death, cruelly and shamefully, in their wrath at the dishonour done to their house.

And still the flow of blood was not staunched. When Callirrhoe came to know how she had been deceived and bereaved, beside herself with rage, she prayed Zeus, by her kinship with the gods, to make her two boys grow up at once to men that they might lose not a day in avenging their father. Zeus nodded consent; and the sons who lay down careless children rose next morning bearded men, stern and strong. Setting out forthwith on their errand of bloodshed, they fell upon Arsinoe's brothers carrying her necklace and veil to Delphi. Acarnan and Amphoterus killed them both, before they knew they were in danger; they went on to root out their father's house.

Thus the fatal gifts at last came to Callirrhoe. But her father, the wise Achelous, would have none of their baneful charm. He bid carry them, after all, to Delphi, to be hung up in the temple of Apollo; and this being done, the curse, passed on through the Cadmean house, was charmed away from the race of Amphiaraus, whose grandson, Acarnan, settled the Acarnanian land, as Cadmus had been founder of Thebes.

The Temple of Apollo at Corinth, Greece, *c.* 540 B.C. Corinth was one of the chief cities of ancient Greece, situated on the Corinthian Isthmus. Its favourable position between two seas raised Corinth in early times to great commercial prosperity.

ECHO AND NARCISSUS

To the river-god Cephissus was born a son named Narcissus, who seemed to his fond mother the most beautiful of children, and anxiously she sought from the blind prophet Tiresias to know his fate.

"Will he live to old age?" she asked; to which the dark-seeing prophet made answer—"If he shall not have known himself!"

What these mystic words meant, time only would show. The boy grew up rarely beautiful, not only in his mother's eyes but in all that were not blind. There was no maiden but cast loving looks upon him; and less favoured youths must envy the charms that made Narcissus vain above all sons of earth. When he had bloomed to the flower of manhood, he was in love with himself alone.

Shunning all who would fain have been his companions, it was his wont to walk apart in solitary places, lost in admiration of the graceful form which he thought no eye worthy to behold but his own. One day, as he wandered through a wood, unawares he was spied by the wood-nymph Echo, who loved him at first sight, but was dumb to open her heart till he should ask its secret. For on her a strange fate had been laid: Hera, displeased by her chattering tongue, took away from her the power of speech unless in answer to some other voice. So now, when Echo slunk lightly among the thickets, shadowing the steps of that beautiful youth, eager as she was to accost him, she must wait for him to speak first, nor durst she show herself but at his desire. But he, given up to his sweet thoughts of self, strolled on silently, and the maiden followed him lovingly, unseen, till at last, as he halted to drink from a cool spring, his ear was caught by a rustle in the branches.

"Who is there?" exclaimed Narcissus, raising his eyes to peer into the dark green shade.

"*There!*" came echoed back; but he saw not who spoke.

"What do you fear?" he asked; and the invisible voice answered—"*Fear!*"

"Come forth here!" he cried in amazement, when thus his words were given mockingly back to him; and still the voice took no shape.

"*Here!*" was the reply; and now glided forth the blushing Echo, to make as if she would have thrown her arms around his neck.

But in the crystal pool the youth had caught another form that better pleased his eyes; and he roughly brushed away the enamoured nymph, with a hard word.

"What brings you?"

"*You!*" she faltered, shrinking back from his frown.

"Begone!" he bid her angrily. "There can be nothing between such as you and the fair Narcissus."

"*Narcissus!*" sighed Echo, scarcely heard, and stole away on tiptoe to hide her shameful looks in the deep shade, breathing a silent prayer that

Narcissus Taken as a Boy to Thiresias. "He shall live to old age – if he shall not have known himself!" From an illuminated edition of *Metamorphoses* by Ovid, late fifteenth century.

this proud youth might learn for himself what it was to love in vain.

When left alone, Narcissus turned eagerly back to that spring in which he believed to have seen a fairer face. Like a silver mirror it lay, shining in sunlight, framed by a ring of flowery plants, as if to guard it from the plashing tread of cattle. On his knees at the edge, he stretched himself over the bright well, and there looked down upon a face and form so entrancingly beautiful, that he was ready to leap into the water beside it. A priceless statue it seemed, of one at his own blooming age, every limb chiselled like life, with features as of breathing marble, and curling locks that hung above ivory shoulders.

"Who art thou that hast been made so fair?" cried Narcissus; and the lips of the image moved, yet now came no answer.

He smiled, and was smiled back to. He flushed for delight, then the face in the water was overspread with rosy blood, its eyes sparkling like his own. He stretched out his hands towards it, and so the beautiful form beckoned to him; but as soon as his touch broke the clear surface, it vanished like a dream, to return in all its enchantment while he was content to gaze motionless, then again growing dim beneath the tears of vexation he shed into the water.

"I am not one to be despised," he pleaded with his coy charmer, "but

Echo and Narcissus, by Nicholas Poussin, 1594–1665. Oil. (The Louvre, Paris, France.) "He was spied by the wood nymph Echo, who loved him at first sight, but was dumb to speak her heart."

105

Metamorphosis of Narcissus, by Salvador Dali. Oil on canvas, 51 × 78 cm, 1934. (The Tate Gallery, London.) The pitying Gods turned Narcissus into the flower that now bears his name.

such a one as mortal maidens and nymphs, too, have loved in vain."

"*Vain!*" resounded the sad voice of Echo from the woods.

Again and again he leaned down to clasp that lovely shadow in his arms, but always it eluded him; and when he spoke entreating it to his embrace, it but simulated his gestures in unfeeling silence. Maddened by so strong allurement of his own likeness, he could not tear himself away from the mirror in which it ever mocked his yearning fancy. "Alas!" was his constant cry, that always came sighing back from the retreats of the woeful nymph. Hour after hour, day after day, he hung over the pool's brink, nor cared to let food pass his lips, crying all in vain for that imaginary object of adoration, till at last his heart ceased to throb with despair, and he lay still among the water lilies that made his shroud. The gods themselves could not but be touched with pity for so fair a corpse; and thus was Narcissus transformed into the flower that bears his name.

As for poor Echo, who had invoked such punishment on his cold heart, she gained nothing but grief that her prayer was heard. Out of sight, she pined away for despised love, till all left of her was an idle voice. And that still haunts the rocks where never since can she be seen by startled eyes; but always she must be allowed the last word.

THE TALE OF TROY
Paris and Helen

The father of the Trojan race was Dardanus, who wandered across the Hellespont into Mysia, and married a daughter of the shepherd king Teucer. Their grandson Tros had a son named Ilus; and on a height by the river Scamander he built a city named Troy, or Ilion, or sometimes Pergamum, the "tower", its people known as Teucrians, Dardanians, or most famously as Trojans. For his new seat Ilus besought of the great god Zeus some sign of favour; and in answer fell from heaven an image of Pallas-Athene which, under the title of the Palladium, was to be treasured as the luck of Troy.

But soon Troy had ill luck, brought upon it by the son of Ilus, Laomedon, a crooked-minded king dealing falsely both with gods and men. He it was who gave walls to the city, and for that task hired Apollo and Poseidon, when, driven from Olympus by the displeasure of Zeus, they had been condemned for a year to serve some mortal upon earth. Poseidon surrounded Troy with strong walls, while Apollo pastured the king's herds in the valleys of Mount Ida. But after their year's service was up, Laomedon denied them the promised reward, driving them away with threats and insults, so that, when restored to their place in heaven, these gods bore a bitter grudge against Troy, by one of them never forgotten.

Before long, Poseidon's ill will was shown, for he sent to lay waste the

Athena. "An image of Pallas-Athene fell from heaven and was treasured as the luck of Troy." Small archaic bronze, sixth century B.C. (National Museum, Athens.)

Laomedon Erects the Walls of Troy.
From an illuminated edition of
Metamorphoses by Ovid, late fifteenth
century.

Poseidon. A detail from Benvenuto
Cellini's golden salt cellar, 1540–1543.
(Kunsthistorisches Museum, Vienna.)
Brother of Zeus and Hades, Poseidon
ruled over the seas and oceans. The
symbol of his power was the trident,
or three-pointed spear, with which he
shattered the rocks, called forth
storms and shook the earth.

land a ravening monster that could be driven away, spoke an oracle, only by the sacrifice of the king's daughter Hesione. She was already chained to a rock as its trembling victim, when to Troy in the nick of time came Hercules, who undertook to deliver her, as he did by slaying the monster among his many feats and labours. For this deliverance Laomedon had promised him a team of matchless horses given by Zeus to his grandfather Tros. But, the monster slain, again this deceitful king broke faith, and Hercules angrily went his way without the horses, being bound to the service of Eurystheus.

Years later, the hero came back to take vengeance for that deceit. He stormed the city, killed its faithless king, and gave Hesione to his own follower Telamon, who carried her away to Salamis in Greece. But at Hesione's entreaty he let her ransom one of her brothers, Podarces, "the swift-footed", who, now under the name of Priam, "the ransomed", became king of Troy.

Priam and his wife Hecuba had many children. The noblest of her sons was Hector, but the comeliest Paris, before whose birth Hecuba dreamed that she bore a firebrand. That dream being interpreted by a seer as foretelling destruction for Troy, Priam and Hecuba agreed to save the city by exposing the helpless babe to death on the heights of Mount Ida; and so was done through the hands of a slave.

But Paris did not die. Suckled by a bear, they say, the child was found alive after some days, and reared among their own sons by the herdsmen of Mount Ida. In this rude life he grew up hearty, handsome, and strong, a

Feast of Peleus, by E. Burne-Jones. Oil on panel, 37 × 110 cm, 1872–1881. (City Museum and Art Gallery, Birmingham, England.) At the wedding of Peleus and Thetis, Eris alone among the immortals was not invited. This slight to the goddess of strife sparked off the Trojan war.

youth of mark above his fellows, though ignorant that he was a king's son. When he came to manhood he did such feats against the robbers of the mountains, that he won for himself the by-name of Alexander, "helper of men". He married the mountain nymph Œnone, and for a time lived happy among the herds, content with his simple lot and humble home.

One day, as Paris fed his flocks in such a leafy glen of Mount Ida, there appeared to him three stately and beautiful women, whom, even before hearing their names, he was aware of as more than mortal. With them came a noble form, whose winged feet and the herald's staff he bore showed him no other than Hermes, messenger of the gods. In their presence the shepherd stood with beating heart and awestruck eyes, while Hermes thus addressed him—

"Fear not, Paris; these are goddesses that have chosen thee to award among them the prize of beauty. Zeus himself bids thee judge freely which of the three seems fairest in thine eyes; and the father of gods and men will be thy shield in giving true judgment."

With this the god put into his hands a golden apple. At the wedding of Peleus and Thetis, parents of Achilles, Eris alone among the immortals had not been bidden to the feast; then the slighted goddess of strife threw among the guests this golden apple, inscribed *For the fairest!* As was her design, three daughters of Olympus had quarrelled to which it should belong; and now they came agreed to take the judgment of that bright-eyed shepherd, who stood before them scarcely daring to raise his eyes till they heartened him with appealing voices.

"I am Hera, the queen of Olympus," spoke the proudest of the three, "and I have queenly gifts to bestow on the humblest mortal. Give judgment for me, and, shepherd lad as thou art, thine shall be the richest realm on earth!"

"I am Athene, goddess of arts," said the second. "Adjudge the prize to me, and thine shall be fame as the wisest and bravest among men!"

"I am Aphrodite," said the third, with an enchanting smile, "and I have gifts sweeter than these. He who wins my favour need only love to be loved again. Choose me for the fairest among gods, and I promise thee the most beautiful daughter of men as thy wife!" Paris might well stand in doubt before three so dazzling claimants; but he did not hesitate long. He gave the golden apple to the goddess of love, who thanked him with a radiant smile, and confirmed her promise by an oath such as not even gods may break. But Hera and Athene turned frowning away, and henceforth were enemies to all the Trojan race.

The glorious vision having vanished, it now seemed to Paris like a dream amid the toils of his daily life, in which he might have forgotten the promise of Aphrodite. As yet he knew no woman fairer than his loved wife. But soon came a change in his fortunes, when he despised poor Œnone, and left her to weep out her broken heart upon the wild mountain side of Mount Ida.

For the first time since his birth, Paris went down to the city of Troy to try his strength in games held there by King Priam. As prize of one of the contests was proclaimed the herdsman's favourite steer, and he could not bear to think of its passing into the hands of a stranger. Not only that prize he won but others, surpassing even the king's sons, his own brothers as they were, had he but known it. They, for their part, might guess him to be

The Judgement of Paris, Flemish school, sixteenth century. (Civic Museum, Udine, Italy.) Paris was set the awesome task of naming the fairest among the goddesses, Hera, Athene and Aphrodite. His choice in favour of Aphrodite, goddess of beauty, led to the abduction of Helen and the Trojan War.

no common clown, that bore himself above them all. One of his sisters, Cassandra, had the gift of divination; and she it was who recognized in this sunburnt mountaineer the child cast forth to die; then his parents were too glad of such a goodly son to remember what had been foretold of him by the oracle.

Thus restored to his birthright, Paris came to stand so high in Priam's favour, that the king sent him to Greece in command of a great fleet, charged to demand that Hesione, borne off by Hercules, should be given back to her home, after many years. Alone Cassandra denounced this expedition, foretelling how a quarrel with the Greeks would bring them against Troy; but Apollo, who had bestowed on her the gift of prophecy, had again cursed it with the fate that her warnings should never be heeded or taken for true.

The Abduction of Helen. From an illuminated edition of *Metamorphoses* by Ovid, late fifteenth century. "When Paris first saw Helen, he forgot all but that enchanting face."

Paris sailed forth, full of hope and pride, on an errand he did not perform. For he turned aside to visit Menelaus, king of Sparta, married to Helen, the most beautiful woman on earth. At the first sight of this handsome stranger, richly arrayed in purple and gold, Helen was ready to forget her marriage vows. And when his eyes met hers, he forgot his true wife Œnone, weeping lonely on Mount Ida, forgot his father's commands, forgot his own honour; he forgot all but the enchanting face which he was ready to take for that of the goddess herself—alas! to be famed for ages as

"The face that launched a thousand ships,

And burnt the topless towers of Ilium".

The honest heart of Menelaus was so trustful that, going upon some expedition, he left his guest with his queen, to steal one another's love by soft words and kindling looks. He was soon to learn how ill that long-haired Eastern prince could be trusted. Before the king came back, Paris had fled, after breaking into his house by force, carrying off its treasures to the Trojan fleet, among them the dearest of all, the wife so little unwilling to follow a new master, that she left behind the young daughter Hermoine she had borne to Menelaus.

With such a prize on board, the love-sick prince no longer minded the mission on which he had been sent by his father. Now that Aphrodite had fulfilled her promise, he gave himself up to dalliance with this fairest of all mortal fair ones. It was long before he steered for Troy to show her with pride to his own people. Spending the stolen wealth of Menelaus in idle pleasure, these two would fain forget their kin and country. Yet Paris went not without warning. As he sailed over a summer sea, of a sudden it grew so calm that the ship seemed nailed to the water, from which rose the sea-god Nereus with dripping hair and beard, to utter fearful words. "Ill omens guide thy course, robber of another's good! The Greeks will come across this sea, vowed to redress the wrong done by thee and to overthrow the towers of Priam. How many men, how many horses I foresee dead for thy sin, how many Trojans laid low about the ruin of their city!"

Venus Presents Helen to Paris. Venus fulfills her promise to Paris when she offers him Helen, the fairest woman in the world. Engraved from the compositions of John Flaxman for *The Iliad of Homer*, published in 1793.

Hector Chides Paris. Engraved from the compositions of John Flaxman for *The Iliad of Homer*, originally published in 1793. Hector gently upbraids his whimsical brother for his lack of vigour, and urges him to battle.

The Gathering at Aulis

Helen's matchless beauty had drawn about her in youth so many hot suitors that they prudently bound themselves by an oath to honour whatever husband might be chosen for her, and to stand by him against any who should wrong his wedlock. So when Menelaus learned how his wife had been stolen, he could call on a host of fellow rulers to take arms for recovering her and punishing that violator of his home. He and his elder brother Agamemnon, king of Argos, sons of Atreus and descendants of Pelops, were the mightiest lords in the Peloponnesus. Agamemnon, husband of Helen's sister Clytemnestra, stood out as greatest above all the kings of Greece; and when he summoned its princes to gather their ships and men for war with Troy, few ventured to slight his command. Two of

The Baptism of Achilles, by Honoré Daumier. From "Histoires Anciennes", in *Le Charivari*, 1842. Achilles, greatest hero of the Trojan War, was the son of King Peleus of the Myrmidŏnes, and of the Nereid, Thetis. At birth, he was baptised in the River Styx to make him immortal. However, as she dipped Achilles in the river, Thetis forgot to wet the heel by which she clutched him, which remained the one mortal spot on his body.

Achilles at Scyros (opposite). While the true women had eyes only for adornments, Achilles revealed himself by snatching at sword and spear. Fresco from Pompeii, first century A.D. (Archaeological Museum, Naples, Italy.)

the chiefs, indeed, held back at first, yet they were the two who in the end would be most famous among the champions of that war.

One of these was Odysseus (*Ulysses*), who, having married a loving wife, Penelope, was loath to quit her and his young son Telemachus for a war which he foresaw as long and toilsome. So when Palamedes, friend of Menelaus, came with Agamemnon's summons to the rocky island of Ithaca, its crafty chief feigned to be out of his mind, in token of which he was found ploughing with an ox and an ass strangely yoked together, and sowing salt in the furrows. But Palamedes, too, was wily. He brought out the child Telemachus to lay him in front of the plough, then the father so carefully turned it aside as to show himself no madman. It is said that Odysseus never forgave that trick, though he seemed to forget it, and that years afterwards he took a chance of working fatal vengeance on Palamedes. But now, betrayed out of his pretence, he had to go with him to the gathering host, for which he soon could enlist a nobler champion.

Achilles was son of Peleus, a mortal married to the goddess Thetis, at whose wedding Eris threw down among the gifts that golden apple to be the seed of so much strife. His mother foretold that either he might die young after heroic deeds, or live long in ignoble ease; and eagerly the boy chose a short and glorious life. She sought to make him invulnerable by dipping him in the water of Styx; then the heel by which she held him remained the one mortal spot in his body. He was brought up with other heroes by old Cheiron, who fed him on the hearts of lions and the marrow of bears, and taught him gentle arts as well as the stern trade of war. Among all his companions he was noted for courage and pride, for generosity and hot temper, as for strength, beauty, and activity that won him such epithets as the "swift-footed", and the "yellow-haired" Achilles.

When the Trojan war was hatching, Thetis, aware that it should lead him to his death, would fain have kept her son away. So she sent him, dressed as a maiden, to be hidden among the daughters of the king of Scyros. There cunning Odysseus sought him out in the disguise of a merchant, who among rich clothes and other womanish gauds carried a store of bright weapons; then, while the true women had eyes only for adornments, Achilles revealed himself by snatching at sword and spear among all those wares. His sex thus disclosed, it was not hard for Odysseus to bring him to the army, leading a band of warlike and devoted Myrmidons from his native Thessaly.

Another service the Ithacan prince undertook in going with Palamedes and Menelaus as an embassy to demand of Priam that Helen should be given back. The king of Troy and his people heard them with amazement, as now for the first time they learned what Paris had done in Greece; and Priam would give no answer till his son came home to speak for himself. For his part, he had to complain of his sister Hesione held captive, for whom Helen might rightly be kept a hostage, if she were brought to Troy. And while the father tried to speak them fair, to the threats of these Greeks the Trojan princes gave back high words, so that

The Sacrifice of Iphigenia at Aulis. On the advice of the seer, Calchas, Agamemnon prepares to sacrifice his daughter to appease the goddess, Artemis. Wall painting from the House of the Tragic Poet at Pompeii, A.D. 63–79. (Archaeological Museum, Naples, Italy.)

they had almost come to blows had not grey heads checked the hot blood of youth. The ambassadors, courteously treated and put under guard against the insolence of the common folk, had to depart without their errand, bearing messages of defiance that made not for peace. As to Hesione, they told Priam how she was long happily married in Greece, and that her son Teucer was among the leaders of the host gathering to take vengeance on Troy.

After long lingering in foreign lands and seas, Paris brought home that bewitching bride, over whom the old king shook his head, and would

114

fain have frowned on the darling son who had so ill done his mission in Greece. But his brothers, bribed by the wealth Paris had stolen from Sparta, and by the smiles of Helen's handmaidens given to those still unmarried, were loud against letting her go back to Menelaus. Their mother Hecuba was set to learn from her own lips whether she followed Paris by free will; and when Priam heard that it was so, he agreed with his sons to defend her against all the power of Greece. His people feared the trials of the war now threatened; and as Paris strode through the streets of Troy, many a stifled curse followed him, who cared not that he brought such woe upon the city; yet even the grey-beards who frowned on Helen could not but turn their heads to look after so lovely a stranger. But the princes were deaf to the ominous warnings of their sister Cassandra. Among them Hector stood out as chief leader, now that his father was too old for war; and of the allies Troy called to its aid, the most illustrious was Priam's son-in-law, Æneas, prince of the neighbouring Dardanians, who had no less a mother than Aphrodite.

Meanwhile, the Greek ambassadors had returned to Aulis, a harbour on the Euripus, where more than a thousand ships were gathered to carry a hundred thousand warriors across the sea. [But the fleet is becalmed and cannot leave harbour. This is the revenge of the goddess Artemis, whose pride has been hurt by Agamemnon having killed one of her sacred hinds in the course of a hunting expedition inland. Artemis will not be appeased without the sacrifice of Agamemnon's daughter Iphigenia. Though horrified, Agamemnon sends his wife Clytemnestra to bring Iphigenia to Aulis, on pretence that she is to be married to Achilles.]

Athene Represses the Fury of Achilles, as he revolts against the tragic sacrifice of Iphigenia. Illustration from Flaxman's designs for *Stories From Homer* by A.J. Church, 1888, London.

Ajax Defends the Greek Ships. Illustration from Flaxman's designs for *Stories From Homer* by A.J. Church, 1888, London. Always at the forefront of battle, Ajax fought with power and force rather than with skill.

Soon arrived Clytemnestra and Iphigenia with her infant brother Orestes; and again the king's heart was wrung by the joyful embraces of his daughter, who could not understand why they called forth no answering smiles. Clytemnestra better knew her husband; and his gloomy looks filled her with suspicion, the more so when, seeking out Achilles, she heard from him that he knew nothing of the feigned betrothal to Iphigenia. Next she fell in with the slave prevented by Menelaus from carrying her husband's second message, and he told how Iphigenia was doomed for sacrifice.

When the queen had wrung all the truth from Agamemnon, loud was she in wrath and woe. The daughter clung about her father's knees, praying for mercy. Achilles burst into the tent, offering to shield her against the whole host already clamouring for her blood. But Agamemnon now stood like a rock against threats and entreaties: he remembered that he was a king as well as a father, nor yet a despot, but one who must consult with those who followed him in war. And Iphigenia, drying her tears, rose to stand upright before him, saying with firm voice—

"Since so it must be, I am willing to die; then shall I be called the honour of Greek maidenhood, who have given my life for the motherland. Let the fall of Troy be my marriage feast and my monument!"

She turned away, her young brother Orestes clasped in her arms,

Achilles and Ajax Playing Dice. Black-figure amphora by Exekias, *c.* 540 B.C. (Museo Etrusco Gregoriano, The Vatican, Rome.) Ajax and Achilles were "the trustiest champions of the besiegers".

Ajax (opposite), by Henri Serrur, 1794–1865. Oil on canvas, 127 × 94 cm, 1820. (Musée des Beaux Arts, Lille, France.) Ajax the Great was massive in stature. Second only to Achilles in bravery and strength, he distinguished himself in the Trojan War.

leaving their mother prostrate on the ground in helpless despair. Iphigenia's last words were a promise to stand still as a lamb when brought to the altar; while Achilles, who had come verily to love this patient victim, spoke hotly of rescuing her by force under the knife of the priest, yet must fear that even his fierce Myrmidons would shrink from violating a sacred rite.

The Grecian host had been drawn up on a plain beside Aulis, where stood the altar of Artemis decked for ceremony. Iphigenia was led forth. Calchas unsheathed his sacrificial knife. The anguished father hid his face. A herald had proclaimed reverent silence, but not a man could speak or move as the noble maid stretched forth her neck to the blade that already glittered above her like the hard eyes of the slaughterer. Then lo! a wonder. Artemis had taken pity on this innocent victim: Iphigenia vanished, borne off by the goddess in a cloud to serve in perpetual maidenhood as priestess of her temple at Tauris. In the maiden's place, a milk-white fawn lay writhing before the altar, sprinkled with its blood. [Artemis is appeased. As the sacrificial victim burns upon the altar, a wind gets up, allowing the fleet to sail for the coast of Troy.]

Clytemnestra heard how her daughter had been carried away, never to see her more. Without waiting to take leave of her husband, she set out for his city of Mycenæ; ill blood rankling in her heart that in later years was to work long woe for the house of Agamemnon.

Many a hero who now hailed the bristling walls of Troy, would never again see wife or child. They had vowed not to cut their hair till these walls fell before them; but little thought the "long-haired Achæans" that the siege of this strong city would take them ten toilsome years.

The Wrath of Achilles

On the Trojan shore, at the confluent mouth of the rivers Simois and Scamander, the Greeks hauled up their ships, placing them orderly in rows, propped on beams and stones, with lanes between the squadron from each city; and each leader lived among his own followers, in tents or in huts of wood and earth, thatched with reeds, so that the camp was like a town, built over against the high-set battlements of Troy. In the midst was left an open space for public gatherings and for the altars of the gods. At either end it was guarded by Achilles and by the huge Ajax, as trustiest champions of the besiegers. Agamemnon, that "king of men", had his quarter, as beseemed, in the centre, among the tents of Ulysses, Menelaus, Diomede, Nestor, and other warriors from all parts of Greece.

Between the city and the camp, the two rivers enclosed an open plain that made arena for many a fray. Again and again the Trojans sallied forth to hot battle beneath their walls. Each army was led on by its champions whirling up the dust in their war-chariots, from which often they would spring down to meet one another hand to hand in single combat, while all the rest stood still to look on, mingling their shouts with the clang of arms.

The Parthenon. Temple of Athena Parthenos on the Acropolis of Athens, the Parthenon was designed in the Doric style. Built entirely of Pentelic marble, it was adorned within and without with colours and gilding and sculptures regarded as the masterpieces of ancient art.

Now one, now the other party got the better, and drove its enemy out of the field. But when years had passed, and many souls of heroes had gone down to Hades before their time, not yet were the Greeks able to break through the walls of Troy. [Nine years the Greeks stay encamped before Troy, enduring pestilence and the deprivations of war. During this time, Achilles and Agamemnon quarrel over the return of a captured Trojan girl, Chryseis, daughter of Chryses, a priest of Apollo, whom the Greeks fear they have offended. Agamemnon returns Chryseis but steals Briseis, another captive Trojan girl, from Achilles. Angry and offended, Achilles vows to fight no more. The ranks lose heart, become restless and speak of repairing to their ships to sail back to their wives and children who await them in Greece. Reproaching, commanding and beating back the deserters, Odysseus manages to quell the rebellion.]

The rout thus stayed, Odysseus eloquently called to his comrades' minds their vows, their hopes, the favourable omens that promised the fall of Troy. Old Nestor also addressed the warriors, bidding them forbear all strife but against the foe. Agamemnon no longer wasted his breath on crafty speech, but plainly ordered battle array. After offering sacrifice to the gods, and taking a meal that for many a man might be his last, the Greek host, as was their wont, advanced silently and sternly in close ranks,

Achilles Bereft of Briseis, by Bertel Thorwaldsen, marble relief. (Woburn Abbey, England, 1803, Bedford Estate.) High-handed Agamemnon seized Briseis from Achilles and so started the dire feud between the two heroes.

wrapt in a cloud of dust, while the Trojans came out to meet them like a noisy flock of cranes, with boastful cries and idle clash of arms. But he who should have led the Achæans on to victory, now sat sullenly in his tent.

The Battles of the Gods and Heroes

The armies being drawn up face to face, ready to set on, Paris, wearing a panther's skin over his bright armour, stepped gracefully forth from the Trojan ranks to challenge the bravest of the Greeks. At the word, Menelaus sprang from his chariot and bounded forward like a lion upon the spoiler of his home. But when Paris, erst brave as beautiful, saw the hero in all the fierceness of his wrong, conscience turned him coward; he flinched from the encounter, and would have shrunk back among the thick of his own people, had not Hector sharply upbraided him for shirking the foe he had brought on their native city by his womanly tricks and graces.

His brother's scorn goaded Paris back to pride; and he nerved himself to fight out the quarrel in single combat with Menelaus, its issue to decide the war. A parley was called, a truce proclaimed, and the two armies ranged themselves about the lists in which that eventful duel should end so much slaughter. From the walls of Troy, old Priam looked anxiously on;

Seated Deities. From right to left: Hermes, messenger of the gods, with his hat in his lap; Dionysus, the youthful god of wine; Demeter, goddess of nature, with her torch; and Ares, god of war. Marble relief, east frieze from the Parthenon in Athens, *c.* 440 B.C. (The British Museum, London.)

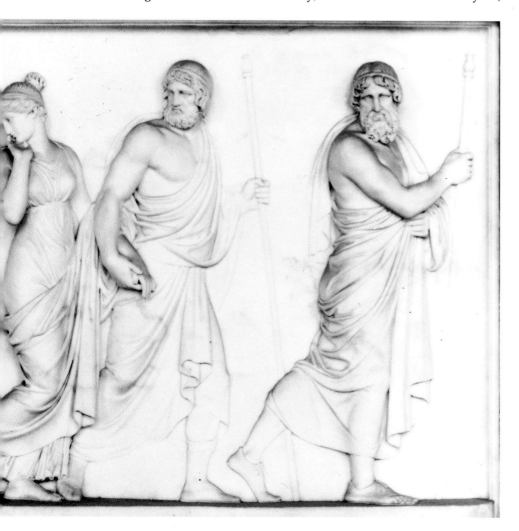

119

The Spoils of War, by David Ligare. Oil on canvas, 152 × 198 cm, 1978–1986. (Private collection.) "Then the Greeks laid Patroclus on a bier . . . Achilles walking with many tears by his side . . . 'I would that I might die this hour, seeing that I could not help my friend . . .'"

and to him came Helen, who, as she sat weaving her story into a web of golden tapestry, had been called to witness the battle between her rival husbands. Sitting by Priam's side, she named to him the chiefs of the Greeks, once her familiar friends, kingly Agamemnon, gigantic Ajax, wise Odysseus; but she looked in vain for her brothers Castor and Pollux, cut off by fate since she left their Spartan home.

When all was ready, Priam turned away, for he could not bear to behold the peril of his darling son. But Helen kept her place, gazing through tears upon her first husband, who now again seemed dear to her in his manly wrath. Lots being drawn for which of her lovers should cast the first javelin, the chance fell to Paris, and her eyes followed the shining dart as it sped through the air to bound back from the Greek's ringing shield. With a prayer to Zeus to guide his weapon well, Menelaus next threw with such forceful aim that the point pierced through shield and armour and garment, and but for drawing deftly back, Paris had felt a deadly wound. As he staggered under the shock, the son of Atreus was upon him with drawn sword. The keen blade splintered against the prince's crest, and broke off short in the hand of Menelaus, who then grasped Paris by the helmet and would have dragged him off among the exulting Greeks. [Aphrodite intervenes to carry Paris away and lay him fainting at Helen's side. Beyond the city walls, meanwhile, the battle rages on. Rivers run red with blood. Again the Greeks face despair, feeling that "the very gods fought for their foe". Despite the appeals of Odysseus, Ajax and Phoenix, whom Agamemnon sends as ambassadors, Achilles still refuses to fight; but he lends his chariot and his armour to his close friend Patroclus, who forthwith launches an attack upon the Trojans. Patroclus is killed by Hector, and Achilles' armour taken as a trophy.]

Hector and Achilles

[On hearing this news, Achilles vows to avenge the death of Patroclus. He makes his peace with Agamemnon and, provided with a new suit of armour by Thetis, strides out to challenge Hector.]

Without more ado they hurled darts that went amiss, then closed upon each other. Achilles, all aflame, burned more fiercely to see that adversary wearing his own armour torn from Patroclus. Ere long his blade found a joint to pierce between neck and throat. Hector fell, gasping out his life with bootless prayer for pious burial. The last words he heard were Achilles' bitter threat that his body should feast the dogs and vultures; and his own last murmur warned the Grecian hero that he too was doomed to die before Troy.

[Achilles then drags Hector's body behind his chariot.]

Within Troy now all was woe and wailing, as day after day the insatiable avenger could be seen dragging the body of its champion thrice round the pile sacred to Patroclus. Pitying gods preserved Hector's corpse from decay, and when twelve days had gone, Zeus was moved to save it from dishonour. He sent Thetis to soften her son's heart that he might agree to let it be ransomed. Then from the walls, in a chariot loaded with

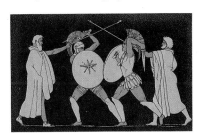

Hector and Ajax Separated by the Heralds. Illustration from Flaxman's designs for *Stories From Homer* by A.J. Church, 1888, London. "Fight no more my sons; Zeus loves you both; and ye are both mighty warriors . . ."

Hector by Jacques-Louis David (1748–1825). Oil. (Musée Fabre, Montpellier, France.) Chief champion of the Trojans, Hector was slain by Achilles in revenge for Patroclus' death.

Obsequies of Patroclus (following page), by Jacques-Louis David. Oil on canvas, 94 × 218 cm, 1778–1779. (National Gallery of Ireland, Dublin.) "But thee, O Patroclus, I will not bury till I bring hither the head and arms of Hector, and twelve men of Troy to slay at thy funeral pile."

Andromache Faints on the Wall.
Engraving from the compositions of
John Flaxman for *The Iliad of Homer*,
originally published in 1793.

rich gifts, came forth old Priam to throw himself at the feet of Achilles, clasping his knees and praying him, as he revered his own father, to give up the body of that noblest son. [Achilles calls a truce to allow Hector's body to be buried with due rites.]

Then at last dawned Achilles' day to die. One spot on the hero's body was alone vulnerable, the heel by which his mother held him when dipped into the water of Styx. To that spot the archer-god guided a chance shaft of Paris; and thus unworthily fell the warrior that had sent so many souls down to Hades.

The Fall of Troy

Still Troy did not yield, for all the heroes battering ever at its gates. Achilles' son, Pyrrhus, showed himself a true branch of heroic stock; but neither for him did the walls fall that had held out against his father. Then Calchas the seer, offering sacrifice, read in the entrails of the victim that Troy would not be taken without the arrows of Hercules, given in legacy to his friend Philoctetes.

[This hero had sailed from Aulis with the rest of the Greeks but, going on shore, was bitten by a snake. Philoctetes becoming demented by the pain, his companions had abandoned him on the isle of Lemnos. Odysseus and Pyrrhus sail to the isle and persuade Philoctetes to come with them, bringing the arrows of Hercules.]

The Death of Achilles (right), by Peter Paul Rubens, 1577–1640. Oil on panel, 107 × 108 cm. (Seilern Collection, Courtauld Institute, London.) Paris, brother of Hector, is said to have killed Achilles, either by one of his arrows, or by treachery.

Ajax and Ulysses Contest the Arms of Achilles. Achilles' splendid arms, "brighter than fire" were wrought by Hephaestus, god of fire. Engraving for an illustrated edition of *Metamorphoses* by Ovid. Published in 1683 in Amsterdam.

No healing could help a wound made by the arrows of Hercules, poisoned in the Lernaean hydra's black blood; and by one of them it was that Paris now met a miserable death.

Again spoke an oracle that Troy could not fall so long as it treasured its Palladium, that image of Pallas fallen from heaven. Again Odysseus showed himself bold as well as cunning. He and Diomede, in beggars' weeds, slunk by night within the walls of Troy, known to none in that disguise save only to Helen, but she, for fear or shame, did not betray her old friends, though well aware that they came on no friendly errand. Her heart was now going back to her true husband, whose feats of arms she beheld daily from the walls; and she even helped his comrades to steal from the temple of Pallas that sacred image. So unhurt they brought the Palladium at daybreak to the camp, to be hailed by the exulting Greeks as a sure sign of victory.

Yet still those oracles seemed to befool the army, against which Troy held out stoutly as ever. When the chiefs could no longer bind their followers to the weary war, Odysseus hit on the device that was at last to make an end. By his counsel they framed a huge horse of wood, moved on wheels, and hollow inside to hold twelve men, of whom he made one, along with Diomede, Pyrrhus, and other chosen warriors. Leaving this fabric full in view, charged with its baleful freight, the Greeks sailed away through the night, as if they had given up the siege in despair; but they cast anchor under the isle of Tenedos, in sight of the Trojan shore.

Those so long cooped up within Troy at first could hardly trust their eyes when in the morning they saw the enemy's camp deserted behind its smouldering watch fires. Then like bees they came swarming out of the gates to spread freely over the fields that for ten years they had trod but in hasty sallies. Nothing held their thankful eyes like that strange shape of a wooden horse: what could it be, and why left behind by the retreating enemy? Some were for dragging it off into the city, even if the gates had to be broken down to give it passage; but others cried for caution, and loudest of all Laocoon, the priest of Apollo, who ran up to warn his countrymen that here must be some deceit. [Declaring that the very gifts of the Greeks are dangerous, Laocoon flings a spear that pierces the wooden horse and causes a rattle of arms within.]

While some spoke of cutting the ominous gift to pieces, and some of hurling it over a rock into the sea, there went a rumour through the throng that drew all eyes away, turned on a prisoner whom certain shepherds had found lurking in the sedge by the shore, and he gave himself up to be led bound before Priam.

[This was Sinon, a young Greek, who gives the Trojans to understand that their enemy, weary of war, has withdrawn. Falsely winning Priam's confidence, Sinon announces that the wooden horse is a gift that must enter the city and be offered in the temple of Athene.]

The Theft of the Palladium. Red-figured Apulian stemless cup by the Diomed painter, early fourth century B.C. (Ashmolean Museum, Oxford, England.) Diomedes and Odysseus carried off the Palladium from the city of Troy, since it was believed that Troy could not be taken so long as the Palladium was within its walls.

Then, lo! a portent seemed to confirm Sinon's lies. As Laocoon now stood in act to sacrifice a steer to Poseidon, over the sea came skimming two enormous serpents, that drew themselves on land and, with hissing heads upreared, slid straight for the altar. They first fell upon the priest's two young sons standing there too scared to fly, till the scaly coils were wound about their limbs. While the other spectators stared in speechless amazement, Laocoon with a cry ran to plunge his knife into those throats already gorging on his boys' flesh; but him also the monsters involved in their loathsome embrace, twisting twice round his neck and his waist, to crush all three, laced together in helpless torment. Laocoon and his sons being thus choked to death, the serpents glided on to hide themselves in the temple of Pallas, without harming any other Trojan, so that they

Laocoon, by El Greco. Canvas, 137.5 × 172.5 cm, *c*. 1610. (The National Gallery, Washington.) Laocoon and his two sons were strangled by sea-serpents sent by Poseidon to punish the priest for his attack on the Trojan horse.

seemed sent as ministers of divine vengeance on the priest who had thrown a spear at that consecrated image.

The cry arose that Laocoon was justly punished, and that the Horse should forthwith be taken in, as an offering grateful to the goddess. The infatuated Trojans harnessed themselves to that fatal machine, dragging it up to the town with songs and shouts of welcome, else at every jolt they might have heard the clash of arms in its hollow womb. They even broke a breach in their wall to let it pass; and, when it was stowed in the temple, all the people gave themselves up to feast and jollity, their weapons thrown aside as no longer needed, and the gates left unguarded on what was to be the last night of Troy.

[At a sign from Sinon, who signals with a torch as darkness falls, the Greek fleet returns to the Trojan shore. The soldiers pour out of the ships to steal up to the walls. Within, Sinon releases the warriors hidden inside the wooden horse.]

Æneas, become Priam's chief defence since Hector's death, was disturbed in his sleep by the pale ghost of Priam's palace, hotly stormed, and as hotly defended. Intent on saving the king, he made his way inside

The Burning of Troy, by Daniel van Heil, 1604–1662. Oil on canvas, 56 × 76.5 cm. "A band of Trojans . . . pale in the glare of their burning homes."

through a secret postern, then sprang towards the highest tower, already shaking under the battering of the assailants. Soon their axes burst open the gate, and in they poured, young Pyrrhus raging like a beast of prey at their head, before whom maids and matrons fled shrieking from court to court, and from chamber to chamber, in vain seeking to escape death or slavery or a worse fate.

The queen Hecuba and her attendants had taken refuge with Priam at his household altar, the old king encumbered with hastily donned armour and weapons he could no longer wield. Here came flying their young son Polites, hard pressed by the raging Pyrrhus, whose spear laid him dead at his father's feet. Crying out to the gods against such cruelty, Priam, beside himself for grief, with shaking hand threw a dart that jingled harmlessly on the rabid warrior's shield, and but challenged him to savage bloodshed. He dragged down the old man, butchering him at his own altar beside the body of his son.

Æneas had come in time to witness this slaughter, which he would fain have avenged. But he stood alone; and the gruesome sight recalled to him his own helpless father in peril along with his wife and child. His comrades were dead or fled; some had even leaped into the flames in the horror of despair. There was nothing for it but to turn while escape was yet open. As he sped away, the glare of the conflagration showed him Helen crouched in a porch, her face muffled from the two peoples to whom she had wrought such woe. Æneas had a mind to slay this curse of his country and hers. But between the sword and its graceless victim came a radiant apparition of his goddess-mother, who urged him forthwith to save his family, since hostile deities were invisibly upheaving the stones of Troy and stirring the conflagration kindled by Achæan hands.

[Amid the confusion, Æneas finds his way to his own house. He gathers up his father Anchises, his wife Creusa and his son Iulus.]

Thus Æneas left his home, picking out dark and devious passages through the burning city, for he, late so fierce in fight, was afraid of every shadow now that these helpless dear ones were in danger at his side. Silently they slunk to a broken gate, but there Anchises cried that he saw the glittering arms of Greeks close at hand; then his son hurried on to plunge into the darkness outside the walls. When Æneus ventured to halt and looked round, he missed his wife, gone astray in their confused haste; and when he reached the temple at which they should meet, Creusa was nowhere to be seen.

Distracted by anxiety, Æneas left the band of fugitives and ran back to the city. Sword in hand, he dashed through smoke and sparks, retracing the line of his flight in a vain search for Creusa, whose name he recklessly kept calling into the darkness. He pushed on as far as his house, to find it on fire and full of plundering foes. He flew to her father Priam's palace in faint hope she might have taken shelter there. Alas! before the temple of Hera, he saw a flock of weeping mothers and children standing captive beside a heap of rich spoil, guarded by Odysseus and old Phœnix. Was this the lot of his hapless spouse; or was hers among the bleeding corpses over which he stumbled at every step? Then suddenly she stood before him, not indeed her living self, but a glimmering and looming shape that struck him dumb for dread. His hair standing on end, he listened aghast to a voice which death inspired with prophecy.

[The ghost of Creusa prophesies that Æneas will suffer long years of exile but that he will find a new kingdom and a royal wife. She bids him not to mourn her death.]

With these words she seemed to glide away. He would have held her, throwing his arms round the beloved neck, but they clasped empty air; Creusa had vanished like a dream.

The night passed in such scenes of agitation and amazement. Day began to break as the hero, still unhurt, made his way back to that temple outside the walls, where in his absence were gathered together a band of Trojans, men, women, and children, pale in the glare of their burning homes. Already dawn showed the walls of the city guarded by its triumphant foes. The ten years' warfare was over, the decree of fate fulfilled. There being no more hope in fight, these hapless fugitives turned their backs on the ruin of Troy, and followed Æneas to the sheltering wilds of Mount Ida.

Thence they gained the seashore, to build ships and launch forth in

The Ruins of Ancient Troy. "The ten years' warfare was over . . . the decree of fate fulfilled." Photographed by Edwin Smith in the 1960s.

Mask of Agamemnon. "That 'king of men' was murdered in his bath by his wife's lover." From Mycenae, *c.* 1580–1550 B.C. (National Museum, Athens.)

Clytemnestra, by Frederick Leighton. Oil on canvas, 1874. (Leighton House Museum, London.) Clytemnestra watches from the battlements at Argos, for the beacon fires which are to announce the return of her husband, Agamemnon.

search of the new home foretold by Creusa's shade. Seven years were they driven here and there upon the sea, for still Juno followed them with her implacable hatred of Troy, enlisting the winds and waves to war against its wandering sons, as is told in Virgil's *Æneid*. But at last, with a choice band of heroes, Æneas landed in Italy, was betrothed to Lavinia, only child of old King Latinus, slew his rival Turnus in battle, and so came to found a second Troy on the banks of the Tiber.

And what was the end of Paris, that winsome deceiver that had brought so much misery on his kin and country? Ere this last slaughter, he had been wounded by one of the fatal arrows of Hercules. While Helen made ready to throw herself at the feet of Menelaus, praying for pardon which was not denied, her ravisher, sick at heart and tormented by pain, had crept away to Mount Ida, seeking out his long-deserted wife Œnone. Her he entreated to forget the wrong he had done her, and to heal him of his mortal hurt by herbs of which she knew the secret. And some say that she did forgive him, after all, and that their old love rekindled in the forest solitudes. But others tell how she bitterly repulsed the man who had wronged her a score of years gone:

"Go back to thine adultress and die!" He turned away miserably to die in the dark woods; and there his body was found by those herdsmen that had been foster-brethren of his happier childhood.

As the flames sank and paled in the dawn, who but Œnone came wandering that way, already half-repentant of her heart's bitterness. She asked the shepherds whose ashes were here burning; and when they spoke her husband's name, with a cry she leapt upon his funeral pyre and perished in the same flames. But Helen went back unhurt to Sparta, she who had brought destruction for her dowry to Troy.

THE HOUSE OF AGAMEMNON
Clytemnestra

Troy had fallen; and the princes of Greece could sail away, each with his share of its spoils. But many of those heroes had no joyful home-coming. Even before leaving Asia they fell out among themselves; and when they launched forth for Greece, it was to steer different courses among the Ægean isles. Some were wrecked or driven astray by a storm on the way. Some came back to find themselves forgotten, or supplanted, and to fall into unnatural strife. Some never reached home, but were fain to abide upon distant shores among barbarous folk. Darkest of all was the fate of Agamemnon, king of men, whose glory had paled on the field beside the prowess of outshining heroes. Better were it for him that he had perished before Troy, like Achilles and Hector!

Never had Clytemnestra forgiven her husband for consenting to the sacrifice of Iphigenia. Sister of Helen as she was, she too played false to the brother of Menelaus, and in the long absence of Agamemnon she took for her paramour Ægisthus, his kinsman unkind, who had meanly stayed back from the war. There was ancestral hatred between these two. Their fathers, Atreus and Thyestes, were brothers, yet did one another wrong to leave a legacy of revenge among their children. Ægisthus had murdered his uncle; and now he usurped his cousin's wife and kingdom, giving out among the people that Agamemnon was dead.

But well the guilty pair knew it was not so, and in fear they looked for the day when the king should come back to his own. They had laid a train of beacons that, blazing from rocky isle to isle, and from wave-washed cape to cape, should bear to Mycenæ the news that Troy was at last taken. There came the night when an exulting watchman roused them to see those signals flashing across the sea—a cheerful sight to other Greeks, but a boding message for Ægisthus and Clytemnestra, who must now face the husband so long deceived, so terrible in his wrath.

Agamemnon's approach was announced: the joyful people poured out, hailing their triumphant king; and foremost came Clytemnestra to greet her lord with feigned gladness and treacherous smiles. While he threw himself prostrate, first of all to kiss his native earth, she looked askance at the captive woman by his side, who was indeed Priam's daughter Cassandra, bowed down by the burden of slavery, and speechless among these men of strange tongue. The queen spoke falsely of forlorn distress in her husband's long tarrying afar from home. Now she welcomed him back, and bid him enter his halls, in which was preparing a feast to mark this happy day.

Thanking the gods for safe return, Agamemnon crossed a crimson carpet spread upon his threshold. One warning cry was raised by Cassandra, whose prophetic eye saw that bright web dyed with blood. No one heeded the muttering captive, taken to be crazy for grief; but she shrank back, refusing to enter the house, through whose walls pierced her gifted sight. And soon her voice was echoed by a dreadful sound from within the palace walls.

Agamemnon had asked for a bath to refresh himself before the banquet; and his wife showed herself busy to serve him. But the traitress threw a mantle of web-work round his head, and quickly twisted it about his sturdy limbs ere he could see who lurked behind the door. Standing thus hooded and caught as in a net, out upon him sprang Ægisthus with an axe, to fell that lordly man like a steer, so that he sank into the silver bath filled with his own blood. Thus unworthily died the conqueror of Troy, lamented loudest by the stranger Cassandra, till she, too, perished by the queen's jealous hatred.

Ægisthus and Clytemnestra openly proclaimed their marriage, and Ægisthus took the kingdom for his own. Agamemnon had left a son, the boy Orestes, and a daughter, Electra.

For them Clytemnestra had no such love as for the vanished

The Return of Agamemnon. "His joyful people poured out, hailing their triumphant king." Illustration from designs by Flaxman and others for *Stories From The Greek Tragedians* by A.J. Church, 1880, London.

The Murder of Agamemnon. ". . . out upon him sprang Aegisthus with an axe . . ." Illustration from designs by Flaxman and others for *Stories From The Greek Tragedians* by A.J. Church, 1880, London.

Iphigenia, her eldest born. Slighted and suspected in their father's house, they were as stepchildren to their own mother. Electra, wise beyond her years, came to learn how Ægisthus had in mind to kill her brother before he should grow old enough to avenge their unforgotten father.

The loving sister saw but one way to save the boy, already past his twelfth year. She charged a faithful old servant of Agamemnon with carrying off Orestes by stealth. They fled from Mycenæ; and the young prince found welcome and refuge with Strophius, king of Phocis, akin to his father by marriage, and out of pity, too, willing to protect him against Ægisthus. Electra was left alone to watch over the hero's tomb, living in her mother's family as a slave-girl rather than a daughter.

Strophius had a son named Pylades, of the same age as Orestes. These two grew up together, sharing their sports and tasks, and coming to love one another like true brethren. They kept side by side in every exercise of virtuous youth, both surpassing all their companions, while neither could nor would outstrip the brother of his heart.

Orestes

The murderer of Agamemnon might well fear Orestes, whose mind was set on avenging his father. He had no secrets from Pylades, and in this undertaking the friends swore to stand by each other for life and death. No sooner had they reached manhood than they set out together on the deadly errand.

To Mycenæ, then, they went in disguise, bearing an urn they were to give out as filled with the ashes of Orestes, that Ægisthus might believe himself safe from his blood-foe. They spent the night in pious rites at the tomb of Agamemnon; and there in the dawn they met Electra coming out to keep fresh her father's memory. Years having gone by since they parted, the brother and sister did not know each other, so when these strangers declared themselves to be from Phocis, she eagerly asked for news of her lost brother, Orestes.

"Alas! he is no more," answered the unknown brother, little thinking how he wrung her heart. But over the urn said to contain all that was left of him, Electra broke into such a passion of grief that now he knew his sister, and had not the heart to keep her deceived. He dried her tears by declaring himself to be no other than Orestes.

Boldly they went up to the palace, and kindly were they received by Ægisthus when he heard their story of the feigned death of Orestes, the man he had such cause to dread. No welcome could be too warm for the bearers of that urn. The guests, unarmed but for hidden daggers, sat down to eat with the king and queen, while Electra made some excuse for sending away the servants. As soon as they were alone together, these strangers started to their feet, Pylades seizing Ægisthus, Orestes his mother; and out flashed the daggers.

"Remember Agamemnon! I am his son and thine. The hour of

Cassandra Raving, painted by G. Rowney and engraved by F. Legat, 1803–1805. (The Boydell Shakespeare Gallery, England.) "No-one heeded the muttering captive, taken to be crazy for grief."

vengeance is come!" These were the last words Clytemnestra heard as she fell by her son's hand beside the body of the usurper. The servants, rushing in at the noise, made no stir to defend their hated master, nor were the citizens loath to be rid of a tyrant.

But soon grey heads were shaken over such a deed: however guilty, a mother's blood shed by her son must surely bring a curse on the city. And when the first flush of his exultation had passed off, Orestes himself began to be moved by remorse. It was a malignant fate that had laid on him such a dreadful duty. At his mother's grave, horror came upon him, so that by turns he raved madly with wild words and glaring eyes, or lay speechless like a dead man, tended by Electra; but neither she nor Pylades could bring him back to his right mind. No other Greek would sit with him at meat, or even sleep under the same roof. Some elders of the people were for stoning him to death, that thus might be averted the anger of the gods. But the most part voted for banishment; and so was Orestes driven forth from the city, accompanied by his faithful friend and his sister.

Bitterly now he reproached the god that had spurred him on to a crime in guise of a pious office. Thereon Apollo appeared to him in a dream, bidding him go into the wilds of Arcadia, and remain there for a year till he should be called before a council of the gods, that might purge him from the stain of his mother's blood.

For a year Orestes wandered, mad and miserable, among desert mountains. He sought the shrine of Apollo, and had laid upon him a heavy task to fulfil in expiation of his sin. He must sail to Tauris in the Scythian Chersonese, and from its temple carry off the image of Artemis, jealously guarded by a rude people and a cruel king.

Pylades was eager to share with him that perilous adventure. In a galley manned by fifty men, they set out for the cloudy shores of the Euxine Sea, whose very name made a word of ill omen.

Orestes at the Tomb of Agamemnon. Orestes and Pylades spend the night in pious rites at the tomb of Agamemnon. Illustration from designs by Flaxman for *Stories From The Greek Tragedians* by A.J. Church, 1880, London.

Elektra and Orestes. Elektra grieves over her father's urn. Illustration from designs by Flaxman for *Stories From The Greek Tragedians* by A.J. Church, 1880, London.

Iphigenia

Orestes knew not how the priestess of that Taurian shrine was no other than his eldest sister Iphigenia, carried away in his infancy from Aulis, where the Greeks would have sacrificed her to buy a fair wind. And Iphigenia, long exiled to serve Artemis among barbarous folk, had heard nought of her kin and country through a score of dark years. No word came to that remote land of the fall of Troy, of the death of Agamemnon, of his son's vengeance. Often she longed for news from her old home and would have welcomed any ship that might carry her back to Greece.

One day as its sad priestess stood gazing across the gloomy waves that made her prison, a band of herdsmen exultingly dragged before her two youths they had caught lurking about the temple. Of foreign speech and dress, they gave themselves out for castaway mariners. With secret joy, her heart thrilled within her when at their first words she knew them for countrymen.

Pylades and Orestes Brought as Victims Before Iphigenia, by Benjamin West. Oil on canvas, 100 × 126 cm, 1766. (The Tate Gallery, London.) "Her heart thrilled within her when at their first words she knew them for her countrymen."

"Unhappy ones, I cannot welcome ye!" she cried in the same speech. "Know ye not the law of Tauris, that every stranger treading its soil shall be sacrificed to Artemis, and alas! by my hands?"

"How can a people that honours the gods have such barbarous laws!" exclaimed one of the captives. "We are cast on this shore by misfortune; we claim pity, shelter, aid from pious men."

"I am Orestes, son of Agamemnon, hateful to gods and men since these hands shed my mother's blood."

"I am Pylades, who aided his friend thus to avenge the great Agamemnon."

A cry rose to the lips of the priestess, as she heard that it was her brother who stood before her. It was all she could do to hold herself back from falling into his arms under the eyes of the Taurians, who stood by in watchful suspicion for his talk in an unknown tongue. Hastily she questioned Pylades, and from him was amazed to learn how Agamemnon died, and how Clytemnestra, and what penance had been laid on Orestes, soul-sick to madness for such a crime.

Could she bear to slay with her own hand the brother she had nursed as an infant, or the friend so devoted to him in his evil plight? In her heart she planned to save both those generous youths; but before her barbarian acolytes, thirsting for their blood, she would not trust herself to let Orestes know who she was. Dissembling her inward feelings for the time, she haughtily ordered the captives to be led to prison in bonds.

But at the dead of night their dungeon door was opened, and in stole Iphigenia. Alone beside the Greeks, she told them her name and birth; and now in turn Orestes had the amazement to hear that his sister still lived, while she for the first time learned of all the woes that had fallen on her father's home. Meanwhile the Taurians were clamouring for the sacrifice of the prisoners; and Iphigenia told with a shudder how it was her duty to officiate at this cruel rite. When she heard that they had a stout and well-manned galley waiting for them on the shore, her ready wit devised a way of escape. Iphigenia went to the king with horrified looks: these captives, she declared, were outcasts so deeply stained in guilt that they would bring pollution to the temple of her chaste goddess. Before they could be rendered an acceptable offering, she must purify them with sea water that washes away all offence of man; and the image of Artemis, too, must be cleansed from the taint brought upon it by the very sight of such malefactors.

The unsuspicious king let it be so, for he had come to look up to the foreign priestess as an oracle. While he and his chiefs stayed at the temple, making ready for that sacrifice, Iphigenia went down to the shore alone, bearing the sacred image, and leading the two prisoners by a cord that bound them fast together. Then soon from the cliffs above rang out a cry of alarm, when a strange ship was seen making out to sea, carrying off victims, priestess, and image.

Men ran to tell Thoas, who wrathfully bid launch his swiftest galley in

Orestes Slays Clytemnestra. "Remember Agamemnon! I am his son and thine. The hour of vengeance is come!" Red-figure amphora from Paestum, Italy, *c.* 340 B.C. (J. Paul Getty Museum, Malibu, California.)

pursuit, and from the cliffs would have hurled stones and darts on the fugitives, tugging hard at their oars, against the wind and tide that washed them back towards the shore. But lo! a dazzling light blinded the king's eyes, and from high overhead pealed out the voice of Pallas-Athene.

"Thoas, it is the will of heaven that these strangers shall go free; for my sister Artemis can no longer dwell among a barbarous people that honour her with human bloodshed!"

The Taurians heard with trembling, and now did not dare to stay the Grecian ship. So Iphigenia brought the image to Athens, to be there worshipped more worthily. And there, when his year's penance was up, the Areopagus was appointed as her brother's place of judgment.

In the temple of Pallas was the court held, a solemn array of gods sitting in the likeness of old men. On his knees at the altar, as beseemed a suppliant, Orestes told his story without deceit, making his plea for mercy on the score of a father's death set against a mother's. The votes were taken by white and black stones cast into an urn. When they came to be counted, white and black, for pardon or punishment, were equal in number. Orestes covered his eyes.

"Stay!" cried Pallas, appearing in her own form. "My vote is still to come." She cast a white stone into the urn; and beneath her ægis held above his head Orestes rose a free man while the angry Furies sank howling into the earth.

Thus absolved, Orestes, the avenger of Agamemnon went home to Argos, where now the people welcomed him to his father's kingdom. They say that he married Hermione, the daughter of Menelaus and Helen, after winning her in mortal combat from the son of Achilles, to whom she had been betrothed. And so these two fought out the quarrel of their sires, a generation after so much blood began to flow for the false queen's fatal beauty.

Orestes Suppliant to Apollo. After the murder of his mother, Orestes was seized with madness, and fled from land to land, pursued by the Furies, until on the advice of Apollo, he took refuge in the temple of Athena. Illustration from designs by Flaxman and others for *Stories From The Greek Tragedians* by A.J. Church, 1880, London.

Offerings to the Dead. Sacrifices had first to be purified with sea water. Illustration from designs by Flaxman and others for *Stories From The Greek Tragedians* by A.J. Church, 1880, London.

THE ADVENTURES OF ODYSSEUS
His Perilous Voyage Homewards

Odysseus, who had left his island home for the ten years' war, was then, after Troy had fallen, ten years on a wandering way back. All those years his faithful wife Penelope waited patiently for news of him, while their son Telemachus grew up to hopeful manhood without having known his father. Meantime, persecuted by Poseidon but protected by the care of Pallas, Odysseus went from one misadventure to another, brought about now by adverse fortune, now by his own fault, again by the folly of his men many of whom perished miserably.

When he set sail homewards with a small fleet of ships, at the very outset Odysseus and his company ran into mishap. Not content with the glory and the spoils they had won at Troy, they must needs land on the coast of the fierce Cicons, whose town they plundered and held a feast on the booty. Their prudent leader was for making off at once; but his careless crews sat gorging and swilling, till the Cicons came back upon them with a fresh force of warriors from the inland parts of their country. The carousing Greeks had to stand to arms for a battle that lasted all day, then at evening were fain to escape on board their ships, with the loss of several men from each crew.

Putting out to sea, they must next content with winds and waves. A storm drove them out of their course and tore their sails to tatters. On the tenth day they made an unknown land, where, going on shore for fresh water, Odysseus sent three scouts to spy out the people of the country. These were the Lotus-eaters, living on a plant named lotus, which so dazed their senses that they cared for nothing but dreamy idleness, in the languid air of that land, where all things always seemed the same, and no stranger had the heart to move away from it who had once tasted its flowery food, freely offered by those mild-eyed melancholy lotus-eaters.

The messengers sent forward had alone tasted of that entrancing food. But when Odysseus saw what a spell it worked on these men, he had them dragged away by force and tied fast on the benches of the ships, while the rest of the crews he hurried on board before they should fall under the same charm, to be bound for ever to a life of inglorious ease.

Toiling at their oars, they left the Lotus land behind, and crossed the sea to fall upon perils of another sort on a rugged shore overhung by the smoke of fiery mountain tops. Here dwelt the Cyclopes, a race of hideous and barbarous giants; in form they were strangely monstrous, each having one huge eye flaming across his forehead; and in nature they were cruelly fearsome as their looks. At an island hard by, Odysseus left his ships safely beached, all but one, with which he himself stood across to the rocky coast of the Cyclopes.

As he was coasting along, there came to view a deep cave, its dark mouth overhung by shrubs, above a yard walled in with rough stones and tree trunks as a fold for sheep and goats. Here was the home of a Cyclops named Polyphemus, so inhuman that he chose to live apart even from his fierce fellows. Drawn ashore by curiosity, the bold hero had a mind to explore this gloomy haunt. His ship left hauled up on the beach to await his return, with twelve of the bravest men picked for companions, he climbed to the mouth of the cave, carrying some food in a wallet, and also a goatskin full of rich wine which he had brought away from Troy, now to serve him better than he knew.

When they reached the cave, they found it full of lambs and kids penned up within, along with piles of cheeses and great vessels of milk and curds. The giant being out on the hills where he herded his flock, these strangers made bold to feast on his stores; then the men were for making off before he came back; but now it was their leader's turn to be

The Blinding of Polyphemus. "And they thrust the stake of olive wood into the monster's eye, for he had but one eye, and that in the midst of his forehead, with the eyebrow below it." Neck of Proto-Attic amphora, *c.* 675 B.C. (Eleusis Museum, Greece.)

reckless, and he waited to see the owner of such wealth, in hope to find him not less generous than rich. Bitterly was he to repent of his rashness.

At nightfall Polyphemus came home, shaking the ground under his tread, and flinging down a crashing stack of firewood from his broad back as he darkened the mouth of the cave. The very sight of this one-eyed monster was enough to scare his unbidden guests into its deepest recess. When he had driven all the ewes and she-goats inside, he closed the entrance with a rock that would make a load for a score of wagons; then before turning in the mothers to their young, he milked them for his own use, setting aside part of the milk to make cheese, and keeping part for his supper. Last, he lit a fire, the glare of which soon disclosed those trembling lookers-on.

"Who are ye?" he bellowed. "Pirates, or traders, or what?"

Odysseus alone had heart to answer, and told his tale of how they were on their way home from Troy, appealing for hospitality in the name of Zeus, the protector of helpless travellers. Without another word, the greedy giant snatched up two of the men at random, to dash them on the ground and devour their bleeding carcasses, washed down by mighty gulps of milk, after which he stretched himself out to sleep.

But there could be no sleep for his luckless prisoners, fearfully aware of the same horrible fate awaiting them in turn. Odysseus thought of falling on the heavy-headed monster with his sword; but how then could they move the stone that barred the entrance? When daylight began to peep in, the giant rolled it away with ease; but when he had driven out his

Odysseus, by Jacob Jordeans, 1593–1678, oil. (Pushkin Museum, Moscow.) "One by one, the prisoners slipped undetected through his fumbling clutches."

flocks, he carefully put it back, shutting up those captives as if by a lid clapped to. And the first thing he had done on getting up was to grab two more of them for his breakfast.

All day the rest lay there in quaking dread, but their artful captain was scheming out a plan to get the better of that cruel host. Within the cave he had left lying a great club of olive-wood, big enough to be the mast of a ship. The end of this Odysseus cut off, and made his men sharpen it to a point and harden it in the fire; then he hid it away in the dirt that lay thick over the floor.

Again the giant came back at evening; again he milked his flock; and again he caught up two of the sailors to make a cannibal feast. Then Odysseus brought to him a bowl of dark-red wine, filled from his goatskin, humbly offering it as a drink fit to wash down the heartiest supper. Polyphemus tasted, smacked his lips, drank down every drop, and asked for more.

Then he rolled over on the ground, stretching himself out to snore off the fumes of the wine. As soon as he was fast asleep, Odysseus heated in the fire the sharp stake he had made ready; then with four men bearing a hand, he suddenly drove it into the monster's eye, turning it round to be quenched in bubbling and hissing blood.

The blinded Cyclops got to his feet with such howls of rage and pain that his assailants fled out of reach, but in vain now he groped and stumbled about to catch them.

For the plotters crouching at the back of the cave now came the question how they were to leave it safely. Their groaning jailer, indeed, pushed away the stone, but he sat down at the entrance, stretching his hands across it to catch them when they should try to slip out, for he thought these men as stupid as himself. But Odysseus had another trick in his bag. With osier withs he tied together the big rams by threes, a man fastened hidden among their fleecy bodies. The biggest and woolliest ram he took for himself to cling on to, face upwards, below its belly.

As soon as it was light, the rams pressed out to their pasture, their master feeling their backs as they passed. One by one the prisoners slipped undetected through his fumbling clutches; then, once got well outside, Odysseus untied his comrades, and, driving along the pick of the flock, they hastened down to the shore, to be joyfully received by their shipmates, who had given them up for lost.

Hurriedly they put their booty on board and launched from the beach.

The next land they made was the floating island of Æolus, king of the Winds, where they found no lack of hospitable entertainment. Æolus and his sons were keen to hear about the siege of Troy, that filled all the world with rumour, so they kept those welcome guests for a whole month of eating, drinking, and talking. When at length Odysseus grew restless to continue his voyage, Æolus did him a rare favour by tying up all the winds but one for him in an ox-hide bag, which he might carry on board. Only the gentle west wind did he leave free to waft the ships straight to Ithaca.

Head of Odysseus. A detail from *The Blinding of Polyphemus by Odysseus,* Greek marble group, by Hagesander of Rhodes and others, from Sperlonga, Italy, *c.* A.D. 25. (Museo Archeologico, Sperlonga, Italy.) Odysseus, King of Ithaca, was a principal hero of the Trojan War, noted for his cunning and craft. Quick-witted and silver-tongued, he side-stepped many a misfortune, and brought his men to safety.

They sailed on then and, for a week toiled in a dead calm. On the seventh day they made the rocky harbour of the Læstrygonians. This people, too, turned out to be cannibal giants, who flocked down in crowds to crush the ships under a shower of rocks and spear the poor sailors like fishes. Odysseus and his men rowed off for their lives, amid the splash of rocks the Læstrygonians pelted at them till they were clear of that fatal haven. This one crew, thus far lucky, but sad for the loss of their comrades, held on till they reached another island. They were so tired that on coming to shore they lay two days without caring to know who lived here. It was indeed the home of the fell enchantress Circe, sister of Medea, a place to which the Argonauts had found their way years before.

[On Circe's isle, a party of Odysseus's men are turned into pigs by a stroke of the enchantress's wand. The god Hermes provides Odysseus with a sprig of the sacred herb *moly*, proof against her spell. Amazed at her failure to work the spell on Odysseus, Circe falls at his feet; she restores his men to human form and provides the weary sailors with fresh clothes and a good dinner.

Taking their leave of Circe, Odysseus and his men sail to Hades,

Circe and her Lovers in a Landscape, by Dosso Dossi, canvas, 100 × 136 cm, *c.* 1525. (The National Gallery of Washington.) Circe, daughter of the Sun, was a charming enchantress accomplished in magical arts. She turned into swine any ill-fated wanderers who landed on her doorstep.

where they encounter the spirit of the blind Theban prophet, Tiresias, leaning on his staff.]

"Odysseus," quoth he, "thy homecoming will be no halcyon voyage, since Neptune bears a spite against the man that blindeth his Cyclops son. Yet all may go well if, when ye reach the Trinacrian shore, ye harm not the herds of the Sun that pasture there. But to slay them will bring wreck on ships and men; and if though thyself should escape in sorry plight, it will be to find thy house full of trouble. And in the end death will come to thee from the sea."

[Odysseus then encounters the spirits of his mother and of Agamemnon, Achilles, Ajax and other heroes at the siege of Troy. Finally leaving Hades, the sailors return briefly to Circe's isle.] Again the enchantress gave them friendly entertainment; but Odysseus she drew aside to ply him with warnings against further perils of his course.

The Siren, by Armand Point, 1897. (Barry Friedman Collection, New York.) The evocative song of the Sirenes lured men to their death.

From Circe's Isle to Calypso's

And well her warnings served him when they again took the sea, still with a favouring wind that soon brought them to the isle of the Sirens, those sisters of enticing song. So sweetly they sang that all who heard them were drawn on shore to where they sat in a field of flowers, blooming among the bones of men thus lured to their death. But on Circe's counsel, before they came within earshot, Odysseus stopped the ears of his men with wax, and made them bind himself fast to the mast, charging them by no means to unloose him, however he might beg or command when his ears were filled with the fatal voices.

The Temple of Poseidon, Greek god of the sea, at Cap Sounion, Greece, fifth century B.C. Photographed by Edwin Smith in the 1960s. "Poseidon bears a spite against the man who blinded his son . . ."

Thus prepared, winged by their oars they flew past the beach on which could be seen the Siren Sisters, and over the waters came their tempting strains, heard by the captain alone.

Their song so thrilled his heart that Odysseus struggled hard to get loose, and by cries and signs would have bidden his men undo the cords; but they tied him up all the tighter, and deaf to him as to the Siren music, rowed their best till they were far out of hearing. Then only they unbound him, and took the wax from their ears; and for once the Sirens had sung their song in vain.

But, that peril hardly passed, another arose before them where the waters boiled with a fierce roaring that made the men drop their oars, staring aghast into the smother of spray and foam. It was all Odysseus could do to hearten them for rowing on, and he durst not tell them the worst he had learned from Circe of this fearful passage, beset by two monsters hungering for the lives of luckless mariners. For now they must tug swiftly and steer deftly between the two rocks, no more than a bow-shot apart. Under the lower rock was prisoned Charybdis, hateful daughter of Poseidon, that three times a day belched out a whirlpool, and three times sucked it back with all that came into its resistless gulp. Still more dreadful was the opposite den of Scylla.

[Though losing six men, the sailors row themselves clear. Tired, hungry and mourning their lost companions, they moor for the night in a harbour on a rocky coast.]

They seemed like to starve, when Odysseus sought a solitary place in which to pray to the gods alone. On coming back, he was startled by the smell of roast meat, and to his wrathful dismay he found the sailors gorging themselves on carcasses of the sacred cattle which they had butchered in guise of a sacrifice. It was too late for him to forbid, nor did his greedy men heed the prodigies that appeared to rebuke their crime, for the very hides of the dead beasts rose and walked, and the joints on the spits lowed as if still alive. For a week they kept up the impious banquet, in spite of all entreaty or warning; till at last came a blink of fine weather to tempt them to their doom.

Meanwhile, Hyperion the Sun-god had made loud complaint in

143

A Fantastic Cave Landscape with Odysseus and Calypso, by Jan Brueghel the elder, 1568–1625, and Hendrick de Clerck. Oil. (Johnny van Haeften Gallery, London.) The lovely nymph, Calypso, lived on the idyllic island, Ogygia, on which Odysseus was shipwrecked.

heaven, threatening to forsake the sky and to shine henceforth down in Hades among the dead, unless he were granted vengeance upon those insolent men that had ravaged his beloved herds. Zeus appeased him by promising swift punishment; and Poseidon had kept an angry eye on that crew ever since the blinding of his Cyclops son. So no sooner were they out of sight of land, than the storm burst upon them afresh. The first squall blew out their mast to crush the steersman in its toppling over; and as the broken hulk tossed ungoverned upon the waves, from the dark sky shot a thunderbolt that shivered it to pieces.

Every man was swallowed up by the raging sea, save only Odysseus, who contrived to catch hold of the mast, and to tie it with other wreckage, making a raft on which he drifted away; for nine days he was carried by winds and waves, whither he knew not, till the tenth night washed his raft on shore.

The hero came thus stranded on the island of Ogygia, where dwelt the divine nymph Calypso, daughter of Atlas. She, like Circe, was an enchantress, but her charms lay in lovely looks and loving eyes; and her wooded island home was as beautiful as its mistress. To a shipwrecked mariner the grotto in which she lived might well seem a blessed haven.

To this solitary abode Calypso welcomed Odysseus with kindness, soon warming into love for the guest who, time-worn and toil-scarred, was still a goodly man in her soft eyes. So well she loved him that she would have him never leave the island; and at first the hero was content to rest here from his weary wanderings. So months sped by, and years, as in a dream. A spell of immortal beauty seemed laid upon Penelope's husband, so that he forgot all but the passing hours of happiness. Yet as time went by, he remembered his own rough island; and often, stealing apart from his charmer, would sit by the shore alone, to gaze over the waves with wistful thoughts of home.

[Odysseus spends seven years on Calypso's isle, half entranced, half yearning to escape. In Ithaca, meanwhile, Penelope, without news of her husband, is pressed to wed one of her suitors. Telemachus, her son, prevails upon Hèrmes to let Odysseus go and continue his journey homewards.]

Much as it went against her heart, Calypso did all she could to speed his departure. She gave him tools to cut down trees, with which he built a raft, and her own garments she brought to make sails for it, and stored his little craft with victuals and skins of wine and water; and she raised for him a softly favouring breeze, when on the fifth day he launched forth, too ready to see the last of that charming hostess.

New Friends in Need

Once out at sea, his sailor-craft came back to Odysseus, long as he had lain idle on land. Steering heedfully by the Pleiades and the North Star, for seventeen days he never shut his eyes nor took his hand from the helm, till the eighteenth dawn showed him welcome land ahead. But now Poseidon made haste to work him ill. The wrathful god lashed up the sea with his trident, calling forth storm winds from every quarter to wrestle round the

Penelope and the Suitors, by J.W. Waterhouse, 1912. (City of Aberdeen Art Gallery and Museums, Scotland.) Wise Penelope kept her suitors at bay by wit and craft.

little raft and whirl it about like thistledown. "Would that I had died illustriously among the heroes of Troy!" was Odysseus' thought, as he felt his frail craft breaking up beneath him.

Before long, however, he saw nothing else for it but to throw off his garments and plunge among the waves.

And now indeed the hero had been lost but for the aid of Pallas, who laid all the winds but one, and let that carry him steadily towards the land. Two days and two nights he kept himself afloat on the swell; and when the third morning broke, a joyful sight of wooded hills close by gave him strength to strike out for dry ground.

At last he was able to drag himself ashore, so battered out of breath and strength that he lay in a swoon, and only after a little was able to kiss the ground in token of thankfulness.

But not yet did he seem safe. Night was drawing on, and the chill wind numbed his weary nakedness. He crawled into a wood for shelter, and made himself a bed of dry leaves, to forget his troubles in such sleep as falls on men who for long have not dared close an eye.

[The island on which Odysseus finds himself is Scheria, inhabited by the Phaeacians, rich traders. To help Odysseus, Pallas guides Nausicaa, the king's daughter, to the spot where he lies asleep. She provides him with food, drink and clothing and leads him into Scheria's walled city. The king, Alcinous, and queen, Arete, receive him kindly.]

This king and his people were so hospitable to a guest, as remembering how they might entertain some god unawares. They did not much trouble the castaway with questions while he ate and drank heartily after his long fast; yet before being shown to a snug bed outside the hall, he told the king and queen of his shipwreck, and how he had been found destitute on the shore by Nausicaa.

[At a banquet in his honour, the blind bard Demodocus entertains the guests with songs of love. Odysseus requests that the bard recount the tragic tale of Troy.]

That, then, the bard sang so stirringly, and so loudly extolled the son of Laertes, as first among heroes of fame, that Odysseus could not keep back his tears. Alcinous, sitting beside him, noted how he turned his head to weep; then this kindly host cut short the song that moved in his guest such painful memories.

"Who and whence art thou, to grieve for the fate of Troy?" he asked; and the answer was—

"I am Odysseus."

Amazed were the king and his lords to hear how this needy stranger, who had sat silent among them, was no other than that illustrious hero vanished for years from the knowledge of men. Eagerly they sought to learn all that had befallen him through those weary years; and half the night he kept them listening to a tale of adventures that would make matter for many minstrels.

But now it seemed as if his troubles were indeed near an end. For if

Ulysses Follows the Cart of Nausicaa. "Foliow thou with the maidens, and I will lead the way in the wagon, for I would not that the people should speak lightly of me." Illustration from Flaxman's designs for *Stories From Homer* by A.J. Church, 1888, London.

Ulysses Weeps at the Song of Demodocus. "So the minstrel sang of the Trojan war, and Odysseus wept to hear the tale." Illustration from Flaxman's designs for *Stories From Homer*, by A.J. Church, 1888, London.

the Phæcians had been friendly and serviceable to the nameless castaway, they had nothing too good for the renowned warrior. Already they had given him bounteous gifts; and furthermore at the king's bidding they heaped for him a treasure of gold and bronze vessels and goodly raiment, to be loaded upon the ship that should bear him home without delay.

The Return to Ithaca

[Odysseus reaches Ithaca. Once more coming to his aid, Pallas meets him on the seashore.]

First helping him, like the prudent goddess she was, to hide away his treasure in the Naiads' cave, she sat down with him below the olive tree to let him know how matters stood in his house, taken possession of by a greedy crowd of suitors for his wife's hand, who would give her true husband no kindly welcome. Penelope, he heard with joy, was still faithful to him, though she had always much ado to put off their importunity. Telemachus had left home in search of his father, and the suitors were plotting to rid themselves of the heir on his return; but the goddess undertook to bring him quickly and safely back. Meanwhile, she advised Odysseus to take refuge with Eumæus, the keeper of his swine, and thence to spy out the state of his enemies before revealing himself. The better to escape their malice, he must be transformed as a lowly beggar.

[Thus disguised, Odysseus is given food and shelter by the swineherd Eumæus in his lowly hut. There, he encounters his son Telemachus. Pallas transforms the beggar back to his own form. Telemachus is dumfounded but incredulous that this is his father.]

At last made to understand that his long-lost sire stood before him in

Penelope, by David Ligare. Wise and faithful wife of Odysseus, Penelope held her many suitors at bay awaiting her husband's return. Oil on canvas, 152 × 198 cm, 1980. (Private collection.)

flesh and blood, Telemachus was so overcome with joy that they might have sat weeping in one another's arms all day. But the wary Odysseus knew that it was a time for deeds rather than words. Hastily telling how he had come to be landed on Ithaca, he questioned the youth as to the number of the suitors who were vexing his wife and eating up his substance. Alas! Telemachus told him, they were too many and too bold to be driven away.

[Once more disguised as a beggar, Odysseus enters his own house and bears the insults that Penelope's suitors hurl at him while a banquet is being held. Later, Penelope sits down with the beggar to hear what news he brings.]

Strange to say, sitting with him in the firelight, she did not know that long-parted spouse, nor did she recognize his voice when she began by asking who and whence he was, and he put the question off by declaring himself a man of sorrows, who would fain not recall his past. Yet she took him at once into her confidence, explaining her woeful plight, and the device by which she had so long warded off the importunity of her suitors, weaving diligently at that costly web but by night secretly undoing the labour of the day.

Glad as he was to learn her faithfulness, not yet would Odysseus reveal to this patient wife that her widowhood was at an end. With his wonted craft, he spun a story of how he came from Crete, and how he had there made acquaintance with Odysseus.

[Penelope is moved to tears by memories of her husband, but resolves to choose as her new spouse one of the greedy suitors.]

One of her husband's feats had been to send an arrow straight through twelve axe-heads set up in a row. To this test she proposed to

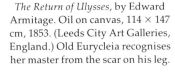

The Return of Ulysses, by Edward Armitage. Oil on canvas, 114 × 147 cm, 1853. (Leeds City Art Galleries, England.) Old Eurycleia recognises her master from the scar on his leg.

Penelope Brings the Bow of Odysseus to her Suitors, by Padovino, 1620s. (National Gallery of Ireland, Dublin.) "Ye suitors who devour this house, making pretence that ye wish to wed me, lo! here is the bow of the great Odysseus. Who so shall bend it . . . him will I follow."

invite the suitors before another sun set; then whichever of them could bend the great bow of Odysseus and rival his unerring aim, him she would take for her new lord.

Let her so do without delay, replied the stranger, for he took on himself to say that before any one of that crew could bend his bow, Odysseus himself would be among them.

[The next day, Penelope appears bearing the huge bow and quiver that a hero gave to her husband many years ago. A handmaid follows with a chest filled with steel and bronze axes.

None of the suitors have the strength to string the great bow. Odysseus steps forward.]

The suitors took for certain that he could make nothing of it; but to their consternation he strung it as lightly as a bard tunes his lyre, and twanged the tight cord so that it twittered like a swallow at his touch. At that moment there came a peal of thunder overhead to stir up his heart; but the suitors turned pale, as the seeming beggar fixed an arrow on the bowstring, and without rising from his seat, he shot it straight through the heads of the twelve axes, not one missed.

With his bow, Odysseus then takes his revenge on the suitors, shooting them one by one. Penelope is struck by disbelief.

Not even yet could Penelope believe that the ragged and gore-grimed beggar was no other than her husband: only some god, she thought, could have so dealt with that throng of oppressors. In vain Telemachus besought her to speak to his father. She turned away her eyes and stood dumb for amazement.

Odysseus bid the bard Phemius strike his lyre to set the servants dancing, sounds of revelry that brought a crowd about the house outside, little aware what had gone on within, but taking it that Penelope's wedding was come at last. Meanwhile, the hero retired with old Eurycleia to the bath, from which he came forth washed and anointed, in goodly clothes, looking like a god indeed, for Pallas had breathed over him an air of more than manly beauty.

Still Penelope was hard of belief that it could be her own husband who sat down before her. To try him, she bade Eurycleia bring out the bed of Odysseus from his chamber.

"Nay," quoth he, "there is no man living can move that bed, unless some god aid him. For I built this house round an olive tree, and the stump I dressed to be the post of my bridal bed, as is known only to me and to thee."

That proof broke down Penelope's lingering disbelief. She threw her arms round her husband's neck, with tears, kisses, and excuses for having been so slow to own him.

Much had the so-long-sundered pair to hear and to tell between them. The whole night would not have been enough for the story of twenty years, had not Pallas drawn out their rapturous hours by her guardian care, holding back the fleet steeds of Aurora beneath the ocean, to lengthen the night after that day when Odysseus came to his own.

CUPID AND PSYCHE
Aphrodite's Rival

Once upon a time a king and queen had three fair daughters, of whom the two eldest came to wed princely suitors. But the youngest, Psyche, was so wondrously beautiful that no one durst woo her, who seemed worthy rather of adoration. Men gazed at her from afar as at a goddess, and the rumour went that this was no mortal maiden, but Aphrodite herself revealed on earth to show her matchless charms in flesh and blood.

So eager was all the world to behold this prodigy, that far and wide the altars of the true goddess stood cold and silent, her chief shrines at Cnidus, Paphos, and Cythera deserted by the crowds flocking to strew flowers under the feet of Psyche. The jealous Aphrodite, seeing herself neglected for such a rival, called on her son to avenge her with his mischievous arrows.

"Inflame her heart with love, but with hottest love for the meanest wretch alive, so that together they may come to poverty and sorrow!"

Ever too ready to play his cruel tricks, young Cupid promised to do his mother's bidding, and flew off to work harm for Psyche. But at the first sight of her beauty he was so amazed that he dropped on his foot the shaft he had made ready for her, and so became wounded by the enchantment of his own weapon. Himself unseen, he loved this mortal as hotly as he thought to make her love some unworthy man.

Aphrodite of Cnidus. Roman copy, after original by Praxiteles, *c.* 340 B.C. (Vatican Museum, Rome.) Aphrodite's shrine at Cnidus was deserted when word of Psyche's beauty spread.

Psyche Raises a Lamp Above the Sleeping Cupid, by F.N. Delaistre, marble, 1785. (The Louvre, Paris.) "The sweetest and loveliest of 'monsters', Cupid himself in the bloom of youthful beauty."

Meanwhile it grieved Psyche's parents that so many came to wonder at but none to wed their youngest daughter. The anxious father sought an oracle of Apollo to know how she should find a husband; and the answer filled him with dread. On the top of a high rocky mountain, he was told, he must leave his daughter alone in bridal array. There should she be wooed by one of whom the very gods stood in fear: she whom men likened to Aphrodite was worthy of no common mate.

Hard was it to part with their daughter thus; but her parents durst not disobey the oracle. At nightfall they led her up the mountain, with a

Psyche Scoured by Cruel Tormentors. The offended goddess, Aphrodite, Cupid's mother, ordered poor Psyche to be scourged until she cried out for mercy. Aquatint, late nineteenth century.

wedding train that seemed rather a funeral, for the light of the torches burned dim, and the songs of the bridesmaids turned to dirges, and poor Psyche was fain to dry her tears with her bridal veil. But having resigned herself to this strange fate as the will of the gods, she strove to comfort her weeping friends. The top of the mountain reached, they quenched the torches, and with tearful farewells left the maiden alone at dead of night as if borne here to her tomb.

When all were gone, Psyche stood shuddering in the chill darkness, full of fear. But soon came a gentle Zephyr that softly wrapped her about and carried her away to lay her on a bed of scented flowers.

Daylight awoke her to look round in wonder. Close at hand, she saw a grove of tall trees, through which flowed a crystal stream, and on its banks stood a house so noble that it appeared the home of a god. The roof of costly woods was borne up by golden and ivory pillars; the floor was paved with coloured marbles, and the walls glowed with pictures inlaid in gems and precious metals. When Psyche ventured to enter, she found vast inner halls more and more splendid the farther she stole on tiptoe, filled with treasures from every part of the earth, and everywhere lit by a gleam of gold shining like the sun. And what seemed most marvellous, all these riches were unguarded, every door stood open, and no living form came to view, as she passed from chamber to chamber, lost in astonishment at the wealth of their unknown lord.

"Who can it be that owns so many rich and beautiful things!" she cried out at length; and soft voices answered in her ear, though as yet she saw no human form.

"All are thine, Psyche! And we are thy servants, appointed to wait on thee. Command us as thou wilt, and it shall be done."

When she was tired of wandering through the palace, and feasting her eyes on its beauty, Psyche took courage to try what such invisible attendants could do for her. Having refreshed herself by bathing in a bath of silver, she took her place at a golden table that was at once spread with the finest fare; then as she ate and drank, soft music arose and a choir of sweet voices filled the room where she sat alone.

So the day passed by as in a dream; and when night fell, she would have lain down on a soft couch spread for her by those unseen hands. Now was she aware of a shadow by her side, and had almost cried out for terror. But her fears were kissed away as she found herself warmly embraced in the darkness, and heard a voice murmuring to her in the kindest tones—

"Dear Psyche, I am the husband chosen for thee by destiny. Ask not my name, seek not to see my face; only believe in my love, and all will be well with us!"

The very sound of his voice and the very touch of his hand won Psyche's heart to this unseen bridegroom. All night he told her of his love, and before daylight dawned, he was gone, since so it must be, promising with a kiss to return as soon as darkness fell.

Thus it was, night after night, that went by in tender speeches and endearments; yet never could she see her lover's face.

The Jealous Sisters

Psyche rejoiced in the love of this husband who came to her only by night; but sad were the long days through which she had to live alone.

[Psyche soon wearies of her life of ease and luxury, and starts to pine in her solitude. Yielding at last to her pleas, Cupid grants her a visit from her two sisters, though he warns her that they will cause unhappiness and makes her promise to tell them nothing about himself. A Zephyr brings her sisters to Psyche the next day.]

Glad was she to see them again, and not less amazed were they by the riches and adornments of her new home. But when eagerly they questioned her as to the master of all this wealth, she put them off with short answers. Her husband, she said, was a handsome young prince who stayed out all day hunting in the woods. And lest she should be tempted by their curiosity to say more, she made haste to dismiss the sisters with costly presents before the hour that should bring him to her arms.

But they, filled with envy of her good fortune, came back next day set

The Stone of Romios, traditional birthplace of Aphrodite, on the coast near Old Paphos, Cyprus. The ancient poets relate that Aphrodite was sprung from the sea, as is suggested by her name, meaning "foam-born".

153

on knowing who could be that great lord so much richer than their own husbands. With caresses they again sought to worm the secret out of her; and this time, forgetting what she had said of him before, she gave out her husband as a grey-bearded merchant, whose affairs called him often away from home. Nor did the sisters fail to note how she contradicted herself, so letting them understand she had something to hide.

Again dismissed with rich presents, the jealous elders were hotter than ever to know the secret of Psyche's marriage. They guessed that this husband of hers must be no mere man, and enviously railed at her for making a mystery of his real name. So they hatched a plot, of which he was well aware, for that night he murmured in her ear—

"Dearest one, beware of thy sisters. To-morrow they will tempt thee to look on me; but that would be the end of our happiness."

With tears and kisses Psyche vowed she would rather die a hundred times than disobey his least wish.

[Though determined to keep her secret, Psyche admits to her sisters that she has never seen her husband and does not know his name. Jealously they put it into her mind that he is a monster who, for all his fair words, will soon devour her. She must kill him while he sleeps. Though torn between love and dread, Psyche makes ready a lamp and knife as night draws near.]

As always, her husband came home with the darkness, and after embracing Psyche, lay down in bed. Curiosity now aiding dread, she made up her mind at least to see what shape he bore. When his breathing told that he was asleep, she rose to light the lamp; then holding it up in one hand and the sharp knife in the other, she stole softly to his side.

A cry had almost burst from her lips, as the lamp-gleam showed the sweetest and loveliest of monsters, Cupid himself in the bloom of youthful beauty, with ambrosial locks curling about his rosy cheeks, and snow-white shoulders on which his wings were softly folded like flowers. At such a sight the knife dropped from Psyche's trembling hand. Beside him lay his bow and quiver, whence she drew out one of the golden-tipped arrows, and in examining it pricked her finger, instantly inflaming her blood with new love for a husband no longer unseen.

Bending over this sleeping form, she would have hastily stooped to kiss him, when in her agitation she let a drop of hot oil fall from the lamp upon his shoulder. Roused by the smart, Cupid sprang up, and at a glance understood all. "Ah, Psyche!" he exclaimed, "thou hast ruined our love. Why listen to thy treacherous sisters rather than to my warning? Now we must part for ever!"

In tearful entreaties she sank before him, and sought to clasp his knees; but he spread his wings and flew into the air without a look of forgiveness. At the same moment, the enchanted palace vanished about her like a dream, then Psyche stood alone in the cold darkness, calling vainly for the love she had lost, with his last words ringing in her ears.

The Council of the Gods. Zeus pleads Cupid's case to which the gods agree. Engraved from the compositions of John Flaxman for *The Iliad of Homer*, originally published in 1793.

Penance and Pardon

Psyche's first thought, as she turned away from the scene of her lost happiness, was to die in despair. Coming to a river bank, she threw herself into its black water; but the pitiful stream washed her ashore on the further side, and she wandered on, hardly knowing where she went.

Psyche went her way alone through the world, everywhere seeking in vain for her vanished love. He, fevered by the pain of his burnt shoulder, or rather by the same grief as gave Psyche no rest by night and day, had taken refuge in his mother's chamber, and lay sick of a wound he durst not own. But a telltale bird whispered in Aphrodite's ear how Cupid had deigned to love a mortal, and hot was her anger to learn this was no other than the very maid boasted on earth as her rival.

In sore dudgeon the resentful goddess tended her son with rating and upbraiding. She threatened to take away his arrows, to unstring his bow, to quench his torch and to clip his wings, that he might no more fly about playing mischievous pranks on gods and men. And though she could not bring herself to punish him as he deserved, all the more eagerly she sought out Psyche for her vengeance.

By leave of Zeus, she sent down Hermes to proclaim through the world that whoever sheltered Psyche should be punished as an enemy to the gods, but seven kisses from Aphrodite herself were offered as reward to whoever gave her up. This proclamation reached poor Psyche's own ears, when, tired of the bootless search for her husband, she was ready to throw herself on his mother's mercy. As a humble suppliant she approached the halls of Aphrodite, where she had no sooner told her name than one of the servants dragged her by the hair into her mistress's presence.

"At last!" the jealous goddess greeted her with mocking laughter. "At last, thou comest to greet thy mother-in-law! Or is it to visit that husband of thine, that lies sick through thy hurting? I have had trouble enough to catch thee; but now thou shalt not go without learning what it is to rival Aphrodite."

Tearing her clothes for rage, she gave over Psyche to be scourged by sore tormentors who stood ready to obey her will. All day, the offended goddess cast about for means of wreaking her spite against the unwelcome daughter-in-law.

[Aphrodite then orders Psyche to sort a mixed heap of wheat, barley, millet and other seeds; gather a handful of wool from the backs of wild, golden-fleeced sheep; and fill an urn with water from the Stygian springs. Psyche accomplishes these apparently impossible tasks, though not without the aid of ants, who help her heap the seeds, a nymph who counsels her to approach the sheep when they sleep, and the eagle of Zeus, who fills the urn for her. Aphrodite is astonished.]

"Art thou, then, a witch, or wicked enchantress, so lightly to finish

Ruins of the Temple of Zeus, Olympia. Photographed by Edwin Smith in the 1960s. Cupid flew to Olympus, begging Zeus to let him marry Psyche.

such perilous tasks?" said Aphrodite mockingly. "But thou shalt be tried still further, my darling, and learn what it is to have the goddess of love for a foe!" she said with irony.

Too tearful were it to tell of all her spite made the hated daughter-in-law and suffer. But those trials had an end when Cupid got to hear of his mother's cruelty, that made him love Psyche all the more. Escaping secretly from his sick-chamber, he flew up to Olympus, and besought Zeus to favour his wedding with a daughter of men.

"Art thou one to ask indulgence at my hands!" quoth that father of the gods, stroking the lad's smooth face. "On which of us, pray, hast thou not played those tricks of thine? I myself have been turned into a bull, a swan, or what not, through thy frolicsome roguery. But we cherish thee kindly as the spoilt child of Olympus, for all thy faults; and if I grant thy prayer, be mindful of the grace thou hast ill deserved."

Forthwith Zeus sent out Hermes to summon a meeting of the gods, to which Aphrodite must come among the rest on pain of high displeasure; and Psyche, too, was brought in with downcast eyes that lit up at the sight of her lost lover among the radiant band. When all were assembled, the father of heaven thus addressed them—

"Gods and goddesses, ye all know this tricksy boy, who has grown up among us, and whose wild pranks I have often had to chastise. Now he is of an age to settle down, with his wanton restlessness fettered in chains of marriage. He has chosen a bride among the daughters of men, to whom he has plighted his troth for weal or woe. What is done, is done; and so be it! Thou, mother of love," he turned to Aphrodite, "do not grudge this alliance with a mortal. To make her the equal of her spouse, I raise her among the gods: henceforth let none despise a child of heaven; and thou, Psyche, take from me the gift of immortality in reward of thy faithful love for Cupid."

With this he held a goblet of nectar to her trembling lips. Psyche drank the wine of the gods; but the charm of deathlessness that ran through her veins was not such a strong cordial as to find Cupid's arms once more thrown round her, in full light of day. All the gods hailed their union; for even Aphrodite ceased to frown when she saw her son's pouting face now bright with smiles, nor could she scorn a daughter-in-law welcomed to Olympus.

So now their wedding feast was held in the home of the gods. Hephæstus cooked the dishes; Dionysus and Ganymede filled the wine cups. The Seasons wreathed the guests with blooming flowers; the Graces scattered perfumes; the Muses sang sweetly to Apollo's lyre; and who but proud Aphrodite herself led the dance! After all their troubles, Cupid and Psyche were made happy; and their first child was a daughter named Joy. Nor was this last of the immortals the least among them in the eyes of generations to come, and in the honour of poets for her that had no priest.

Cupid and Psyche, by Francois Gerard, 1770–1837. Oil. (The Louvre, Paris.) Cupid was so entranced by Psyche's beauty that he dropped one of his arrows on his own foot.

INDEX

INDEX

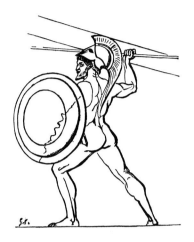

The Four Horae, goddesses of nature and the seasons.

ACKNOWLEDGEMENTS

Birmingham City Museum and Art Gallery, England: 84 (top); The Bridgeman Art Library, London: 17, 19, 44, 62, 70–71, 86, 139, 142, 144; The Bridgeman Art Library, London/ Giraudon, Paris: 25 (top), 40, 43, 57 (top), 62, 96–97, 105, 157; The British Museum, London (by courtesy of the Trustees): 38 (top and bottom), 46 (left), 119; Christie's, London (sale 2 July 1991, lot 7): 47; The Cleveland Museum of Art (Gift from J.H.Wade): 60 (bottom); E.T. Archive, London: 6, 9, 12, 22, 24 (top), 55 (bottom), 61, 83 (top), 85 (top and bottom), 87, 109, 113, 116 (top), 138; Galleria d'arte Forni, Bologna: 110; Fotografica Foglia, Naples: 33, 49, 84 (bottom), 114; National Tourism Organisation of Greece (London): 8 (both), 14 (bottom), 55 (top), 94, 130 (top), 82; Harari & Johns Ltd, London: 28; A.F. Kersting, London: 93, 103, 153; David Ligare, California: 34–35, 120, 147; Mansell Collection, London: 41, 42, 45, 50, 57 (bottom), 150, 151, 152; The Map House, London: 80 (bottom), 99; The Montreal Museum of Fine Arts (Donation of Miss Olive Hosmer, photo Christine Guest MMFA): 74; Phillips Fine Art Auctioneers, London: 128; Scala, Florence: 12–13; Mrs Olive Smith, Saffron Waldon: 13, 15, 23, 60 (top), 65, 77, 81 (both), 106 (bottom), 107 (bottom), 129, 143, 155; The Tate Gallery, London/© DACS 1992: 106 (top); National Gallery of Art, Washington D.C.: 7 (Andrew W. Mellon Collection), 27 (Chester Dale Collection), 127 and 141 (Samuel H. Kress Collection); The Wedgwood Museum, Barlaston, Stoke-on-Trent, Staffordshire, England (by courtesy of the Trustees): 5; Woburn Abbey, Bedfordshire, England (photo Forschungsarchiv für Römische Plastik, Cologne): 26–27, 102; Woburn Abbey, Bedfordshore (by kind permission of the Marquis of Tavistock & the Trustees of the Bedford Estate): 118–119.